Wittenberg Vs. Geneva

Wittenberg Vs. Geneva

A Biblical Bout In 7 Rounds
on the Doctrines that Divide

Brian W. Thomas

An imprint of 1517.the Legacy Project

Wittenberg Vs. Geneva: A Biblical Bout In 7 Rounds on the Doctrines that Divide

All scripture quotations, unless otherwise indicated, are taken from the NET Bible® copyright ©1996–2006 by Biblical Studies Press, L.L.C. All rights reserved.

Scripture quotations from the English Standard Version™, copyright © 2001 by Crossway Bibles, a publishing ministry of Good News Publishers. Used by permission. All rights reserved.

All quotations from the Book of Concord, unless otherwise indicated, are taken from the Concordia Triglotta of 1917.

All quotations of Reformed Confessions and Catechisms were taken from the Center for Reformed Theology and Apologetics (www.reformed.org).

Published by:
New Reformation Publications
PO Box 54032
Irvine, CA 92619-4032

Printed in the United States of America

Library of Congress Cataloging-in-Publication Data

Library of Congress Control Number:

ISBN: 978-1-945500-43-5 Hard Cover
ISBN: 978-1-945500-37-4 Soft Cover
ISBN: 978-1-945500-42-8 E-book

NRP Books is committed to packaging and promoting the finest content for fueling a new Lutheran Reformation. We promote the defense of the Christian faith, confessional Lutheran theology, vocation and civil courage.

Back Cover Photo by Dave Johanson

Table of Contents

Acknowledgments

This book began to take shape in my mind nearly seventeen years ago when I happend across a worn out copy of *The Proof Texts of the Catechism with a Practical Commentary*, edited by Dau and Graebner and published in 1920. It is now held together by duct tape and has become one of my favorite books as it lays out the Christian faith by exploring the scriptures, unafraid of challenging interpretations that run contrary to the Bible. At the time, I had recently made the journey to Wittenberg (Lutheran) by way of Geneva (Presbyterian), and was excited to share with others not only why I had made such an ecclesial shift, but more importantly, how this move had transformed my life. When my Reformed friends wanted to explore Lutheranism futher from a biblical vantage, I had very little to commend them outside of my little worn out copy of the *Proof Texts*; and since it had long been out of print, I began to photo copy sections pertinent to our discussions. "Wouldn't it be great if someone wrote a book that scripturally explored these differences?" I thought to myself. Unfortunately, no one heard me. So this is the book that I had always hoped someone else would write.

I want to thank my former professors at Concordia University, Irvine, for taking the time to respond to my questions and providing me with helpful resources along the way, especially Drs. Mike Middendorf and Rod Rosenbladt. I also would like to thank my friend, colleague, and mentor, Dr. John Bombaro, for his invaluable insight, editorial advice, and late night discussions that made this work far better than it otherwise would have been. Many readers have improved this work with their corrections and comments, and I want to particularly thank Gloria Himmelberger and Joanne Helms for their hard labor in pouring over early manuscript drafts. I would like to pretend it was a labor of love.

The majority of this work was written in San Diego, California, and I wish to express my gratitude to the members of Grace Lutheran Church, who supported and encouraged me in this endeavor. Additionally, I want to thank the librarian and staff at Westminster Theological Seminary in Escondido, who granted me visiting scholar access and helped tremendously in sourcing and suggesting solid Reformed works to study.

Lastly, I want to thank my supportive wife and daughters who patiently experienced many Saturdays with me being only tangentially present even when I was technically present in the house working on "the book."

Brian W. Thomas
Feast of Pentecost, 2015

Foreword

Given the large Creedal overlap of confessional Calvinism and confessional Lutheranism, one would think that there would be a plethora of books and other sources devoted to the simple question, "So what exactly are the differences between these two?" But there are not.

On the Lutheran side, one finds one chapter in Hermann Sasse's *Here We Stand* devoted to this, but not a lot else. When I was a student at the old LCMS seminary in Springfield, IL, it was required of us to purchase Louis Berkhof's dogmatics for our basic course in systematic theology. So far as I know, this did *not* become the norm for today's Confessional Lutheran seminarians. Correlatively, our Francis Pieper will almost certainly be on the bibliography of a "truly Reformed" seminary's dogmatics course, but almost certainly will *not* be required reading.

The layman who asks the simple question about our differences is advised to compare our dogmatics books—a Herculean task at best.

Happily, Lutheran pastor Brian Thomas has tackled this simple question in his book, *Wittenberg Vs. Geneva*. While not the easiest of reading, it is completely accessible to lay readers.

Pastor Thomas' presentation is based on key verses—the best way, according to the Reformers, to argue theological issues. In careful dealing with these key verses, the author walks the reader through the basics, all the while acknowledging where we do *not* disagree—an (unfortunately) rare attribute on the part of Confessional Lutheran authors.

Fully documented for those who wish to consult the primary sources, this book not only answers the key questions with regard to the disjunctions between our camps, it does so by way of actual Biblical passages. I wholeheartedly recommend Pastor Thomas' new book for these (and other) reasons.

Dr. Rod Rosenbladt
Professor of Theology and Christian Apologetics
Concordia University, Irvine

Introduction

In the book, *Mere Christianity*, C.S. Lewis likens the Christian church to a large house with many rooms, each representing a different tradition of the one, holy, catholic, and apostolic Church. While his desire was to draw people into the hallway for discussion, he encouraged his readers to settle down in one of the rooms. "But it is in the rooms, not in the hall, that there are fires and chairs and meals. The hall is a place to wait in, a place from which to try the various doors, not a place to live in."[1]

I did not grow up in the church; therefore, I took Lewis' advice by exploring the Christian house quite thoroughly as a young man, trying various doors in search of a room to call my own. I eventually settled in the Presbyterian room for several years, becoming acquainted with their confessions, catechisms, and popular writers (past and present). It was here that I began to read the works of Martin Luther, Phillip Melanchthon, and Martin Chemnitz. Slowly my confidence in Calvinism began to wane, leading me to cross the hall and enter the Lutheran room, where I remain to this day and serve as one of her pastors.

I am often asked, "Why Lutheranism?" My answer, "I am a Lutheran because I believe it is the most biblically faithful room in the house." When this has been asked by a resident of the Reformed room, a discussion on the topics of Baptism, the Lord's Supper, or Predestination inevitably follows. The difficulty for me as a Lutheran pastor has been the lack of resources to recommend to those who desire to dig deeper on specific areas of disagreement. There are many fine Lutheran publishers, and there is no shortage of good introductions to Lutheranism. But between the very basic

---

[1]Lewis, *Mere Christianity*, xv.

introductions on the one hand, and intimidating technical dogmatic works on the other, there is a dearth of popular material to aid biblically literate Christians in exploring the differences between the two magisterial traditions of the Reformation. By contrast, and to their credit, there are numerous Reformed pastoral theologians who have written scholarly, yet readable, books promoting Calvinism.

No two cities influenced the Western world more than Wittenberg and Geneva during the Reformation period. Wittenberg stood at the very epicenter of Martin Luther's reforming work. Geneva became the home from which John Calvin would shape the life and thought of the Protestant Church. In this book I am not concerned with the two reformers as individuals, though each receives generous citation throughout; but rather, the doctrinal stance of the traditions that bear their names. For both traditions the final authority is neither Luther nor Calvin, but Scripture alone. Therefore, the goal of this book is to provide a biblical defense of the key doctrines that have divided Lutheran and Reformed churches for nearly five centuries. To use Lewis' analogy, it is an invitation for those residing in the Reformed room to enter the hallway for a healthy biblical conversation with their Lutheran neighbors, pugilism aside..

The terms "Reformed" and "Calvinist" will be used synonymously; however, they have become diluted in the era of the "young, restless, and Reformed," to include a wide assortment of evangelicals that include Baptists and nondenominational ecclesial networks that do not formally adhere to any of the classic Reformed confessions like the Westminster Standards or the Three Forms of Unity. For this reason I have largely restricted my polemical sparring partners to Reformed writers who are not only popular and respected within their own circles, but are confessionally faithful to classic Calvinism. Furthermore, the astute reader will soon discover that I have engaged the works of Presbyterian pastor and theologian, R.C. Sproul, more than any other. Sproul has published countless biblical and theological works at both the scholarly and popular level. Since he is widely known, respected, and accessible, I have enlisted him as a contemporary Reformed champion.

Whenever doctrinal differences arise, Reformed theologian Michael Horton notes two dangers: (1) to eliminate the hallway, assuming that our room is the only one in the house and (2) to go in the opposite direction toward a shallowness that loiters in the hallway and never lives in any room.[2] While the Lutheran room is certainly not the only one, I heartily believe it offers the best view of the Bible in the house. As we move through each chapter, it is important to remember Lewis' ecumenical advice, "When you have reached your own room, be kind to those who have chosen different doors and to those who are still in the hall."[3] This does not eliminate the "sweet science" of debate, but it does couch it in a friendly and enjoyable atmosphere.

Pre-fight Rules: Hermeneutical Protection at All Times

Before treating the relevant biblical passages in the chapters that follow, it is important to acknowledge that both Lutherans and Calvinists are in general agreement on two fundamental hermeneutical principles that will prove essential for this study.

1. *Scripture Interprets Scripture.* Sproul writes, "What is unclear or obscure in one place may be clarified in another. We are to interpret the obscure in light of the clear, the implicit in light of the explicit, and narrative in light of the didactic."[4] This, of course, does not mean that God has revealed all things, nor does the Bible answer every question we may desire to know.

2. *Literal Sense.* Our goal is to seek the plain or literal sense of meaning from the Bible like any other book, following the rules of grammar, genre, etc. Sproul cites Luther approvingly on this, "The Holy Spirit is the plainest Writer and Speaker in heaven and on earth. Therefore, His words can have no more than one, and that the most obvious, sense. This we call the literal or natural sense."[5]

I highlight these two because as you consider scriptural points of contention, I want you to ask, "Which room applies these principles faithfully and consistently?"

---

[2] Horton, "Whose Orthodoxy?," 16.

[3] Lewis, *Mere Christianity*, xvi.

[4] Sproul, *Grace Unknown*, 56.

[5] Sproul, *Grace Unknown*, 57.

Atonement

For Whom Did Christ die?

For whom did Christ die? I agree with Michael Horton, in his most recent defense of Calvinism, that this question is clearly addressed in Scripture and carries enormous theological and practical implications.[6] Unfortunately, we come to very different conclusions regarding the answer. Calvinists argue that Christ died only for the elect.[7] In other words, the objects of Christ's death are always, and only, believers chosen by God before the foundation of the world (Eph 1:3–6). Reformed apologists assume that if Christ died for the sins of the entire "world", then all would be saved since God is sovereign and his saving purposes cannot be thwarted.[8] For example, Presbyterian pastor and scholar R.C. Sproul sets up a straw man argument when he argues that universal atonement will naturally lead to universalism (a belief that everyone will be saved), as if universalism is the only alternative.[9] While the Calvinist position is logical and internally consistent, it comes up short in the light of clear passages of Scripture.

In this first round, I will provide an exegetical and theological critique of the Calvinist concept of limited atonement (also known

---

[6]Horton, *For Calvinism*, 80.

[7]Westminster Confession VIII, 4.

[8]Sproul, *Chosen by God*, 205.

[9]Sproul admits that the majority of those holding to a universal position do not actually support universalism, *Grace Unknown*, 165.

as "particular redemption"), and demonstrate that the Bible clearly teaches that God sent His Son (1) to die for the sins of the entire world (universal atonement) and (2) that God desires that all sinners would repent and believe in the Gospel (universal grace).

The Nature and Extent of Christ's Death

John 1:29

On the next day John saw Jesus coming toward him and said, "Look, the Lamb of God who takes away the sin of the world!"

John the Baptist makes a clear and unambiguous declaration regarding the extent of Jesus' redemptive mission—he takes away the sin of the "world." In light of John's extensive usage of "world" (*kosmos*) within the context of salvation, the plain and natural reading of this passage is that "world" means "all fallen human beings."[10]

Palmer attempts to defend the Calvinist position by noting that the Bible often uses the words "world" and "all" in a restricted or narrow sense.[11] This is certainly true. We find "world" used geographically (Luke 2:1–2) as well as hyperbolically (John 12:19). Nevertheless, the immediate context, as well as the repeated use within a particular writer's corpus, helps determine use and meaning.

Alternatively, some Reformed writers argue that texts referencing Christ's saving work containing the expressions "the world," "all men," "all nations," and "every creature" are used by New Testament writers to correct the error that salvation was for the Jews alone. In other words, Jesus died for Jews and Gentiles alike without ethnic distinction, but it should not be understood that he died for all of humanity without exception.[12] Certainly Jewish exclusivity was an issue in the early church, as addressed by Paul in his letter to the Galatians, but, once more, context will dictate use and meaning, and we find no evidence within John's Gospel to force such a narrow definition; in fact, we find the very opposite.

---

[10]See *TDNT* 3:867–98

[11]Palmer, *Five Points of Calvinism*, 52.

[12]Steele and Thomas, *Five Points of Calvinism*, 46.

Both arguments ultimately fall prey to *eisegesis*, which is to say, forcing the text into a predetermined system, rather than accepting the natural reading. I wonder if the Calvinist would be willing to apply the same logic to the word "all" in Romans 3:23 (for *all* have sinned and fall short of the glory of God)? Does "all" refer to the elect alone? Is it simply to distinguish Jew from Gentile, or does it refer to "all" humanity? Reformed commentators unanimously agree it is the latter. All means all.

John 3:16–17

For this is the way God loved the world: He gave his one and only Son, so that everyone who believes in him will not perish but have eternal life. [17]For God did not send his Son into the world to condemn the world, but that the world should be saved through him.

The object of God's love is the "world," and the sending of the Son was for the purpose of saving the "world." Verse 17 makes it unmistakably clear that "world" here means the fallen world, for it is the same world that is under God's condemnation, which is not limited to a particular group of people (elect or ethnic). Long respected as one of the greatest defenders of Calvinism on the atonement, John Owen (1616–1683) treats this passage by retranslating it: "God so loved his *elect throughout the world* that he gave his Son with this intention, that by him believers might be saved."[13] His alteration of the biblical text is quite astonishing. The scriptural warnings against adding to, or subtracting from, God's Word seem *apropos* to such exegesis (Deut 4:2; Prov 30:6; Rev 22:18–19).

1 Timothy 2:3–4

Such prayer for all is good and welcomed before God our Savior, [4]since he wants all people to be saved and to come to the knowledge of the truth.

---

[13]Owen, *The Death of Death*, 214, emphasis mine.

Titus 2:11

For the grace of God has appeared, bringing salvation to all people . . .

2 Peter 3:9

The Lord is not slow concerning his promise, as some regard slowness, but is being patient toward you, because he does not wish for any to perish, but for all to come to repentance.

In these passages, Calvinists restrict the word "all" (*pantas*) to mean "all kinds of people" or simply "all the elect." Sproul offers two possibilities. First, following Owen, he retranslates 2 Peter 3:9 to read, "God does not will that any of us (i.e. elect) to perish."[14] Since Peter is writing to believers, Sproul reasons that God's patience and desire is for elect believers only to reach repentance.

The second possibility for Sproul is to divide God's will into special classes (decretive, prescriptive, and dispositional). In this case, God is not willing (*in the dispositional sense*) that any should perish. According to Sproul, the verse simply speaks of God's common grace and benevolence for humanity. Just as a human judge who sentences a guilty person to prison does not enjoy the task, so God takes no pleasure in sentencing the sinner to hell.[15]

The Calvinist's interpretation of these, and similar passages, falls subservient to the doctrine of predestination, which we shall cover in the next chapter. While Lutherans heartily affirm that God does not take pleasure in the death of the wicked (Ezek 18:23; 33:11), Sproul's interpretation runs contrary to his own logic when you consider that he also advocates double predestination—God not only elects unto salvation, but unto reprobation (i.e., those who will be lost). How could God from eternity "decretively" consign a large portion of humanity to hell before they were even created, while "dispositionally" desiring they would come to saving knowledge of His Son, who did not actually atone for their sins? Such a conclusion pits God's will against itself.

---

[14]Sproul, *Chosen by God*, 197.

[15]Sproul, *Grace Unknown*, 169–70.

The Reformed make an unusual distinction between "common grace" (general and common to all humanity) and "special grace" (redemptive and effectual for the elect alone). To define the concept of common grace, Reformed theologian Louis Berkhof writes:

> It is seen in all that God does to restrain the devastating influence and development of sin in the world, and to maintain and enrich and develop the natural life of mankind in general and of those individuals who constitute the human race . . . It is understood, however, that these privileges can be called common grace only in the sense that they do not constitute special, in the sense of saving, grace.[16]

Common grace is an error of categorical distinction.[17] God certainly restrains sinners from doing all the evil that they could commit, but this does not fall into the biblical category of *grace*; rather, this is category of the *law*. God's word does not merely speak about justice and mercy, it actually judges and forgives, kills and makes alive (2 Cor 3:6). Steven Mueller notes, "God speaks words of judgment and grace: words that are Law and Gospel."[18]

Lutherans like Mueller recognize that the proper distinction between the law and gospel is necessary, because each has an absolutely different content, purpose and effect in the lives of people. The law is the word of God that commands people to do what is right according to God's own moral standards. Mueller elaborates:

> Every person in the world is familiar with the Law of God in some manner. They may not be consciously aware that it is *God's* Law, but it is present in their lives nonetheless. It is written on the hearts of all people (Rom 2:14–15). Whether from the internal voice of the

---

[16]Berkhof, *Systematic Theology*, 435–36. Where the Reformed also see God's common grace in terms of general blessings, such as rain, food and drink, clothing and shelter, etc., the Lutheran tradition would speak of God's providential care in creation.

[17]Reformed theologian, John Frame, admits that he does not know of any place in scripture where *grace* is used in this manner, thus he prefers the terms *common love* or *common favor*, *Salvation Belongs to the Lord*, 112–13.

[18]Mueller, *Called to Believe, Teach, and Confess*, 55.

conscience, from the governing authorities, or from the rules that guide our interpersonal relationships, people are constantly confronted by issues of right and wrong, or rewards and punishments.[19]

What the Reformed refer to as "common grace" is actually the civil-political dimension of God's Law, which concerns the laws in society that govern the outward actions of its populace. The civil use of the law is an extension of the basic moral framework that God has built into the fabric of creation itself, including humanity and the service of government (Rom 2:15, 13:4). Luther thus spoke of unbelievers being "civically righteous." The first function of the Law is to curb sin (i.e., restrain the devastating influence and development of sin and evil).

The gospel on the other hand is the proper category for "grace", as it is the good news of God's favor freely given for all through the life, death, and resurrection of Jesus Christ. In the Old Testament it is given in the promise of the Messiah who was to come. Paul says that the ministry he received from the Lord was to "testify to the good news of God's grace" (Acts 20:24). In other words, grace is not an abstract attribute or wish of God; it is always connected to the work of the Redeemer.[20] Thus, Paul can say that salvation is grounded in God's grace alone, apart from works (Eph 2:8–9). The term grace (*charis*) in the Bible always denotes God's gracious disposition or favor.[21]

I belabor the point because the Reformed locate God's will for the salvation of all humanity and the universal call of the gospel (1 Tim 2:4) under the banner of God's common grace, while simultaneously affirming that he has excluded a large portion of humanity from the get go (reprobation), making no provision for their salvation (limited atonement). Even if the reprobate were to hear the Gospel call to repent and believe in Jesus Christ, it would not be an earnest call (dispositional will), since it can have no effect but to further condemn. Such thoughts do not even remotely resemble the biblical concept of grace, especially when the Westminster Confession adds,

---

[19]Mueller, *Called to Believe, Teach, and Confess*, 59.

[20]Mueller, *Called to Believe, Teach, and Confess*, 68.

[21]See also Pieper, *Christian Dogmatics*, 2:7–17.

"Others, not elected, although they may be called by the ministry of the Word, and may have some common operations of the Spirit, yet they never truly come to Christ, and therefore cannot be saved."[22]

I collectively emphasize the three biblical passages above because they are not dealing with a common or generic concept of God's love, but a very specific one centered in the death of Jesus Christ and his desire for all to come to saving knowledge and trust. While the first tactic of Calvinism is to divert our attention to other texts where the word "all" does not mean all of humanity, they still fail to demonstrate that "all" does not mean all in the context of these specific passages.

2 Peter 2:1

But false prophets arose among the people, just as there will be false teachers among you. These false teachers will infiltrate your midst with destructive heresies, even to the point of denying the Master who bought them. As a result, they bring swift destruction upon themselves.

Peter warns of false teachers and destructive heretics denying Christ who "bought" them. This verse proves troublesome for Reformed interpreters, because inextricably tied to Calvinism's doctrine of election are two others—"irresistible grace" and the "perseverance of the saints". In this redemptive scheme, Christ died only for the elect, and once a person comes to faith (proving they are elect), they cannot lose their salvation. But here Peter writes about apostates who deny Jesus, while simultaneously asserting that such people were bought by Jesus' shed blood. Either the Calvinist position is in error (since they readily acknowledge these apostates are non-elect), or the verse is more complicated than it naturally reads. How does the Calvinist respond?

Presbyterian pastors James Montgomery Boice and Philip Graham Ryken argue that the best approach is to think of Peter as describing what these false teachers "claimed" rather than what they had actually "received" from Jesus.[23] We should read the verse, in their estimation, as a hypothetical. This is certainly a convenient option

---

[22]Westminster Confession X, 4.

[23]Boice and Ryken, *Doctrines of Grace*, 129.

if you desire to fit it into an *a priori* atonement theory. However, when confronted with the actual text (this passage or the letter as a whole), we have no reason to believe that Peter switches from fact to hypothetical, only to switch back to fact, as he continues to disparage these false teachers. Boice and Ryken have chosen an improbable reading of the text that begins with Calvinist assumptions and makes the text perform unnaturally.

Scottish-born Calvinist, John Murray (1898–1975), takes another approach. He argues that either "master" (*despoten*) is not referring to Jesus or that "bought" (*agorazo*) is not used here in a redemptive sense.[24] While *despoten* is used a few times to refer to earthly rulers (cf. 1 Tim 6:1–2; Titus 2:9; 1 Pet 2:18), all other references are used of Christ or God the Father (cf. Luke 2:29; Acts 4:24; 2 Tim 2:1; Rev 6:10). In a strikingly similar passage in Jude, we read: "For certain people have crept in unnoticed who long ago were designated for this condemnation, ungodly people, who pervert the grace of our God into sensuality and *deny our only Master and Lord*, Jesus Christ" (Jude 4 ESV, italics mine). If Jesus is the referent in Peter's use of *despoten*, what alternative do we have, but to understand *agorazo* as a synonym for Christ's death, especially in light of the New Testament's repeated use of it redemptively, "You were bought with a price." (1 Cor 7:23).[25] Jesus died for all, even those who deny him.

1 John 2:2

And he himself is the atoning sacrifice for our sins, and not only for ours only but also for the whole world.

For proponents of universal grace and atonement, this passage is so clear it seems beyond comprehension to interpret it otherwise. Christ's death is not only the propitiation for believers' sins, but for the "whole world" (which, by default, includes the non-elect). However, Calvinists take great pains to explain away a simple reading. For example, Murray suggests that it was important for John to stress the "ethnic universalism of the gospel and therefore of Jesus' propitiation

---

[24]Murray, *Redemption: Accomplished and Applied*, 250–56.

[25]See also Matt 13:44; 1 Cor 6:20; Rev 5:9, 14:3–4.

as the central message of that gospel."[26] The phrase "whole world," according to Murray, simply means that Christ's propitiation extends to every nation, kindred, people, and tongue, but in no way should we understand this to mean the whole world of humanity as falling within the scope of Jesus' death.

I heartily affirm that the gospel is for all nations (Matt 28:19), but the notion that we must restrict John's scope of "whole world" to mean the elect of every nation is not only a forced reading, it fails to take into consideration how John continues to use the word "world" throughout this letter. Just a few verses later, John describes the world that Jesus redeemed, "Because all that is in the world (the desire of the flesh and the desire of the eyes and the arrogance produced by material possessions) is not from the Father, but is from the world" (1 John 2:16). In his concluding remarks he adds, "We know that we are from God, and the whole world lies in the power of the evil one" (1 John 5:19). Clearly, the "world" that John conceives—lustful and in the power of the evil one—cannot refer to ethnic exclusivity or the elect in general, but encompasses the whole world of fallen humanity, not to mention creation itself. According to John, the extent of Jesus' sacrifice knows no such limits.

Thus far we have looked at several passages that clearly teach, from a Lutheran perspective, the universal grace of God and extent of Christ's death for the sins of the entire world. We now turn our attention to those passages that Reformed theologians do rely upon to positively promote their position.

John 6:37–39

Everyone whom the Father gives me will come to me, and the one who comes to me I will never send away. [38]*For I have come down from heaven not to do my own will but the will of the one who sent me.* [39]*Now this is the will of the one who sent me—that I should not lose one person of every one he has given me, but raise them all up at the last day.*

---

[26]Murray, *Redemption*, 73. Sproul similarly contrasts "our" with "whole world" to suggest that it is a contrast of Jew and Gentile vice believers and unbelievers, *Grace Unknown*, 176.

Sproul writes, "There is no uncertainty here. The work of redemption accomplished by Christ as our surety is no mere possibility or potentiality. It is a certainty."[27] To this I respond, "Amen!" Lutherans also affirm John 10:11, "I am the good shepherd. The good shepherd lays down his life for the sheep." But just because Jesus emphasizes his sheep in one particular passage does not compel us to reject, limit, or alter the meaning of other clear passages that speak of Christ's redemptive work universally.

In John's Gospel, Jesus volunteers to go with the officers sent by the chief priests to arrest him, asking them to leave his disciples alone. John's commentary is significant. "Jesus replied, 'I told you that I am he. If you are looking for me, let these men go.' He said this to fulfill the word he had spoken, 'I have not lost a single one of those you gave me'" (John 18:8–9). Here we go back to our first hermeneutical principle: interpret Scripture with Scripture. A universal understanding of God's grace encompasses both the passages that narrow in focus (sheep) and those that widen (world).

John 17:9

I am praying on behalf of them. I am not praying on behalf of the world, but on behalf of those you have given me, because they belong to you.

Here in the "high priestly prayer" Calvinists are quick to point out that Jesus does not pray for the world, but for those whom the Father has given him. Jesus is clearly praying for his disciples; this is not in dispute. Does this force us, as Calvinists argue, to support a limited atonement since Jesus limits this one recorded prayer to believers?[28]

First, just because Jesus specifically prays for his disciples here does not mean he never prayed for unbelievers. His prayer for his executioners, "Father, forgive them for they know not what they do," likely embraced those who were not elect (Luke 23:34). To be sure the text does not give us evidence either way, but we do know at

---

[27]Sproul, *Grace Unknown*, 176.

[28]Sproul, *Grace Unknown*, 175.

the time of the prayer they were certainly not among his followers. I pray daily for my two daughters, but this in no way limits my love, concern, or prayer for other children throughout the world. But let us assume that Jesus did not pray for the non-elect. Paul certainly did as he urged that supplications, prayers, intercessions, and thanksgivings be made for "all" people, which includes civil authorities in power (1 Tim 2:1–2).[29]

Secondly, though Jesus' prayer is here limited to his disciples, as we read further we learn that his love for the world is not so confined. He also prays for the work of his disciples in the world. He has given his disciples his sanctifying Word (vv. 8, 14, 17) and is sending them into the world just as the Father sent him (v. 18), so that the world would come to faith through their words that testify of him (vv. 20, 23). This hardly sounds like a prayer that restricts the grace and work of the Son to a select few.

Third, I find it interesting that Calvinists are comfortable expanding John's use of "world" in this passage to refer to the non-elect, when they are unwilling to do so in the other Johannine passages we have considered. This strikes me as inconsistent.

Objective and Subjective Justification

Calvinists bind the extent of the atonement to its effect, while conceding that Jesus' death was sufficient for the whole world; however, it is only effectual for the elect. If anyone for whom Jesus died is not ultimately saved, the Calvinist reasons that Christ's death was to no avail. A repeated line of Reformed rhetoric states that anyone who argues for unlimited atonement makes salvation only potential or possible, but never actual.[30] While this may be true of synergists, it is not so for Lutherans.

---

[29]Calvinist scholars attempt a way around this by arguing that "all" men here means, "all types or kinds of people," but I find this to be a forced reading and an inconsistent use of scripture. Additionally, Calvinists pray for their families, friends, and others without knowing whether or not they are elect. For a novel Reformed exegetical approach, see Baugh, "Savior of All," 331–40.

[30]Horton, *Christian Faith*, 516–17.

One of the key theological distinctions that Lutherans make to resolve this tension is that of "objective" and "subjective" justification. Objective justification describes the extent of Christ's saving work. Mueller explains:

> By his holy life, death, and resurrection, Christ Jesus has atoned for the sin of the whole world. His work is sufficient payment for every single human being and all of our sins. No one is excluded from his gracious work. There is no one for whom he has not died.[31]

In light of Christ's objective work, Paul concludes "in Christ God was reconciling the world to himself, not counting their trespasses against them" (2 Cor 5:19). God has declared all sinners justified in His eyes for the sake of Jesus, who took away the sins of the world. Yet we agree with the Reformed that not all people universally enjoy the benefits of God's pardon in Christ—now or in eternity. Nevertheless, as Mueller adds, "Christ's death for the sins of the world is an objective fact whether we believe it, reject it, or are ignorant of it."[32]

The application of God's justification in Christ Jesus is not universal or general, but individual and personal. Subjective justification is the work of Christ, applied to and received by an individual in faith, through God's means of grace. Mueller continues, "Objective justification applies to all people, but those who reject the Gospel do not receive the benefits or blessings of that justification. They have chosen to exempt themselves from the gifts that God has given them in Christ."[33]

We can illustrate the objective and subjective nature of justification this way. During the Vietnam War many young men evaded the draft or deserted military service by moving to Canada or other countries for safe haven. Under penalty of federal conscription laws, they could have been prosecuted for such actions had they returned to the country. Following the war, President Carter declared amnesty for all who had evaded the draft. This declaration of amnesty was

---

[31]Mueller, *Called to Believe*, 233.

[32]Mueller, *Called to Believe*, 234.

[33]Mueller, *Called to Believe*, 235.

valid even though many remained in self-imposed exile. If we imagine President Carter had sent U.S. ambassadors to Canada and other foreign countries urging citizens to return home to enjoy their freedom, we can begin to grasp how the apostle Paul understood his own vocation as an ambassador of Jesus Christ, going into a world of objectively reconciled sinners and pleading on Christ's behalf, "Be reconciled" (2 Cor 5:19–20).[34] Here the objective, historical reconciliation which Christ accomplished at Calvary is brought to sinners in what Paul calls the "message of reconciliation."

The completed act of atonement comes to us as good news, not advice, and the appropriate response to this good news is to believe it. "What must I do to be saved?" the jailer asked Paul and Silas (Acts 16:30). Their answer, "Believe in the Lord Jesus." The saving work had already been accomplished for the jailer; he was simply to trust that it was so for him.

The reception of Christ's meritorious work by faith alone (subjective justification) is something Lutherans must highlight, lest we are accused of being in league with synergists in turning faith into something which we contribute to our salvation. For Lutherans, faith is the pure gift of a gracious God. Faith is, as Luther often stated, the receiving organ like an outstretched hand that takes hold of a gift. Likewise, we can have confidence in our salvation, because it does not depend upon us in the least. As Forde remarks:

> The faith by which one is justified is not an active verb of which the Old Adam or Eve is the subject; it is a state-of-being verb. Faith is the state of being grasped by the unconditional claim and promise of the God who calls into being that which is from that which is not. Faith means now having to deal with life in those terms. It is a death and resurrection.[35]

Calvin, too, is in agreement that "as long as Christ remains outside of us . . . all that he has suffered and done for the salvation of

---

[34]This illustration has been in a file of sermon notes I have kept for over a decade and I am uncertain to whom I should give credit.

[35]Forde, *Justification by Faith*, 22.

the human race remains useless and of no value for us."[36] The role of
faith as passive reception, a mere hand, not only safeguards God's
full credit in saving us by grace alone, but also provides comfort for
those who are concerned about the quality or strength of their faith.
It is what faith grasps—the object of faith—that matters, no matter
how firm or weak the grip. Rather than looking to our faith for assurance, the faithful look to Christ, the Lamb of God who takes away
the sin of the world.

The Implications of Limited Atonement

In the opening of this chapter, I quoted Michael Horton who said the
extent of the atonement carries enormous theological and practical
implications. I will close with two implications that result from the
Reformed position.

The first implication is the uncertainty it places upon the
believer. You simply cannot know if Jesus died for you, because it
is impossible to probe the hidden will of God to find out if you are
among the elect. In a very real sense, it forces the believer to turn
inward to one's faith or to good works as the fruit of faith to confirm
that they are in fact righteous in God's eyes (more will be said on this
in chapter 7). If you interpret the universal passages as the Reformed
do, then you cannot ultimately believe your sins are forgiven on the
basis of the objective promises revealed in texts like the ever-popular
John 3:16.

On the other hand, if Jesus did in fact die for the whole world,
then you can know with certainty that he died for you, because you
are a part of the world. And this is not only true for you, but for
everyone. Calvinism requires the believer to assent to the possibility that Christ died for them, but not the actuality. Faith must be
more than a receiving hand, because there is no certainty of what it
is grasping. For the Lutheran, all God's promises find their yes and
amen in Christ Jesus (2 Cor 1:20).

The second implication follows the first. If one denies universal grace, they are directed away from the objective means of

---

[36]Calvin, *Institutes*, 3.1.1.

grace—Word and Sacrament—to the effects of faith. For this rea-son, among others, there is little emphasis in the Reformed tradi-tion upon Baptism and the Lord's Supper as performative rites that accomplish what God's Word says, namely, the forgiveness of sins, life, and salvation. Consequently, Baptism does not enjoy the same kind of identity making significance that it has in Lutheranism. Likewise, the Lord's Supper is celebrated infrequently, and when it is, the stress is often laid upon the believer's worthy reception rather than Christ's comforting promise, "*Given . . . shed . . . for you.*" Once more faith is turned upon itself, leading many to pietism or despair. These two negative implications turn positive when we trust God to apply the objective and universal nature of Christ's work through His Word and Sacraments.

Predestination

Double, Double, Toil and Trouble

It may come as a surprise to some readers, including Lutherans, that our tradition possesses a very robust doctrine of predestination. Admittedly, it does not feature as prominently in our theology as it does in Calvinism. However, both traditions share much in common when it comes to predestination and election. The major division, and thus the purpose of including this chapter, lies with the Calvinist concept of the double decree—an election unto damnation—as the logical flip side to an election unto salvation. Because of this impasse, the emphasis of this chapter will be a comparative exegesis of Romans 9:6–24, the primary passage Calvinists cite in support of their doctrine of reprobation.

The Confessional Lutheran Position

The only confessional treatment of election is found in Article XI of the Formula of Concord, which was included to prevent future disagreement and to counter synergistic opponents who had arisen from within Lutheran ranks, as well as crypto-Calvinist influences that had made inroads into Germany in the latter half of the sixteenth century.[37]

---

[37]For this article's background and summary, see Bente, *Historical Introductions*, 195–208.

The authors of the Formula begin by defining the biblical terms used in the doctrine of election before moving on to a more comprehensive treatment. First, they distinguish and define the terms "foreknowledge" and "election." God's foreknowledge means that God sees and knows everything that is or will be, everything that happens or will happen, whether it is good or evil, because all things exist in the presence of God, whether they are past or future, and nothing is hidden from him.[38] God's foreknowledge applies to both believers and unbelievers. The eternal election of God, however, does not apply to both, but instead only to the children of God, who are chosen and predestined to eternal life, before the foundation of the world (Eph 1:4–5). In distinguishing between these two terms, we note several points of interest.

First, God is not the author or cause of sin and evil.[39] Our Reformed brethren emphasize the same in their confessional writings.

Second, God's eternal election not only foresees and foreknows the salvation of the elect, but is the very *cause* of our salvation and all that pertains to it, founded solely upon the gracious will and good pleasure of God in Christ Jesus. Melanchthon taught that the entire number of those who are to be saved are chosen (*electus*) for the sake of Christ (*propter Christum*), and we should seek no other cause.[40] It is here that we join the Reformed in rejecting the synergistic conception of the *intuitu fidei*, the false notion that God elects us to salvation based upon foreseen faith.

Third, this doctrine will comfort Christians only when viewed in light of the Gospel promises found in Scripture.[41] Predestination presents a mystery of God's love, and it is preposterous to imagine we could ever penetrate God's secret council. Luther said this doctrine is strong wine that should not be given to children. Thus, we are wise to heed Moses' counsel, "Secret things belong to the Lord our God, but those that are revealed belong to us and our children forever" (Deut 29:29).

---

[38] Formula of Concord, Solid Declaration, XI, 4, *Triglotta*, 1063.

[39] See also Augsburg Confession, XIX.

[40] Melanchthon, *Loci Communes* (1543), 172.

[41] Formula of Concord, Solid Declaration, XI, 13, *Concordia*, 634.

Fourth, following the sequence of Paul's logic in Romans 8:28–30, the formulators summarize what God in "his purpose and counsel has ordained" in eight succinct points:

1. Through the atoning work of Christ the human race has been redeemed and reconciled with God;
2. The benefits of Christ's work are given through the Word and Sacraments;
3. The Holy Spirit works efficaciously through these Means of Grace;
4. God justifies all who believe in Christ;
5. God promises to sanctify all believers;
6. God promises to defend and protect all believers in dangers of temptation;
7. He will support the good work done in them to the end;
8. He will finally save and glorify in eternal life those whom He has elected, called, and justified.[42]

Lastly, when Lutherans speak of election, we are careful to confine the doctrine to those who are saved, that is, predestination unto salvation. This view is called "single predestination." Preus defines this well, "Predestination simply means that everything God has done in time to save us and make us His children and preserve us in the faith, he determined in Christ to do for us in eternity. So my salvation is not the result of any whimsical actions or reactions of God, but of His eternal purpose for me."[43] The doctrine of election is therefore good news, and for Lutherans, pure gospel.

The Calvinist Double Decree

By way of contrast, Calvin defines predestination in a twofold manner:

We call predestination God's eternal decree, by which he compacted with himself what he willed to become of each man. For all are not

---

[42]Formula of Concord, Solid Declaration, XI, 15–20. I've relied here upon Bjarne Teigen's summary translation, *I Believe: A Study of the Formula of Concord*, 18.

[43]Preus, *Theology of Concord*, 82.

created in equal condition; rather, eternal life is foreordained for some, *eternal damnation for others*. Therefore, as any man has been created to one or the other of these ends, we speak of him as predestined to life or to death.[44]

Likewise, the Westminster Confession—while wisely urging "great prudence and care" when discussing this doctrine—places God's decree as the principle cause of those marked for hell. "By the decree of God, for the manifestation of his glory, some men and angels are predestined unto everlasting life, and others are *foreordained to everlasting death*."[45]

Behind this understanding of double predestination is a limitation of God's grace for all humanity called "particular grace." If, as the Calvinist believes, Christ did not die for the sins of the whole world, but for the elect alone, then logically election must be two-fold—unto salvation and reprobation—where reprobation is defined as, "God's choice of who will be lost."[46]

Lutherans find such a decree repugnant and contrary to Scripture. We gladly receive all that Scripture teaches on this subject, but stop where it stops, refusing to speculate on matters that have not been revealed. For example, Luke writes in Acts 13:48, "As many as were appointed to eternal life believed." He does not add, however logical it may seem, "as many as were appointed to eternal damnation did not believe." Rather the blame is placed upon the crowd's unbelief because they rejected God's Word (v. 46). This is not an isolated text, but is consistent with the entirety of the New Testament.

Sproul is correct that single predestinarians refuse to draw the inference of what he believes to be the inescapable logic of an election unto reprobation, but not because we desire to "sidestep logical consistency" or have a particular "antipathy to logic in theology," as he puts it, but because the biblical writers leave such matters alone.[47]

---

[44]Calvin, *Institutes*, 3.21.5, emphasis mine.

[45]Westminster Confession III, 3, emphasis mine.

[46]Frame, *Salvation Belongs to the Lord*, 179.

[47]Sproul, "Double Predestination," lines 53–54.

Sproul seems far more confident in his own logical consistency than Paul who is humbled by such contemplation:

> Oh, the depth of the riches and wisdom and knowledge of God! How unsearchable are his judgments and how fathomless his ways! For who has known the mind of the Lord, or who has been his counselor? (Rom 11:33–34)

In the spirit of fairness I must mention two common Lutheran misconceptions of Calvinism when it comes to this doctrine.

First, it is anachronistic to saddle John Calvin with the rationalism that his students would later manifest as they took the raw matter of his *Institutes of the Christian Religion* and applied logic, such as Sproul advocates, to demonstrate the consistency and coherence of their theological system. McGrath notes that Calvin's heirs were concerned with metaphysical and speculative questions, especially as these relate to the nature of God, his will for humanity and creation, and above all the doctrine of predestination, which he believes assumed the status of a controlling principle.[48] While this may be true of some within the Calvinist tradition, I feel it is a stretch to say the same of Calvin himself. Horton reminds us, "Just as Luther's strong defense of predestination in *The Bondage of the Will* was provoked by Erasmus' *Freedom of the Will*, Calvin's lengthy discussions of the subject were responses to his critics."[49]

Lutherans have often portrayed Calvin as if he wrote about nothing else than predestination, which is far from the truth. The topic is not dealt with in the *Institutes* until the third book, following a lengthy treatment on the life of faith. The doctrine is completely absent from the *Genevan Confession* of 1536, and only receives passing mention in connection with the church in the *Geneva Catechism* of 1542. As Calvin's students moved beyond his position, so Lutherans must also acknowledge the fact that many of our own

---

[48]McGrath, *Reformation Thought*, 129–30. Horton, among other Reformed scholars, refutes the notion of predestination as their central dogma, *The Christian Faith*, 315.

[49]Horton, "Getting Past the TULIP," 63.

seventeenth and eighteenth century dogmaticians strayed from the biblical teaching of our confessional fathers.[50]

Second, many Lutherans believe that Calvinists approach the elect and reprobate in a symmetrical manner. This may be true of supralapsarians or hyper-Calvinists, but it is not the case for those who adhere to the Reformed confessions. Here God's election is viewed in an active-passive relationship. While God is the active agent in positively bringing the elect to faith, he merely passes by the reprobate, leaving them in their sin and unbelief, as the Belgic Confession confirms:

> We believe that all the posterity of Adam, being thus fallen into per-
> dition and ruin by the sin of our first parents, God then did manifest
> himself such as he is; that is to say, Merciful and Just: Merciful, since he
> delivers and preserves from this perdition all whom he, in his eternal
> and unchangeable council, of mere goodness hath elected in Christ
> Jesus our Lord, without respect to their works; Just, in leaving others
> in the fall and perdition wherein they have involved themselves.[51]

What of Luther? Sproul provides no evidence to support his claim that "virtually nothing in Calvin's view of predestination was not first in Martin Luther."[52] Those who contend that Luther walked lockstep with Calvin on the double decree typically cite Luther's diatribe with Erasmus, *The Bondage of the Will*, as proof of their assertion. What goes unmentioned is this work is not a systematic presentation of Luther's doctrine of predestination, but rather, a debate on the doctrine of original sin and the spiritual impotence of bound sinners in contrast to Erasmus' semi-Pelagianism.[53] There

---

[50]See Preus, *Theology of Post-Reformation Lutheranism*, 2:96–99.

[51]Belgic Confession, XVI.

[52]Sproul, *What is Reformed Theology?*, 139. It is astonishing that so many Reformed theologians have contributed to the myth that Luther was a "stal-wart Calvinist," as one writer put it. It is not only anachronistic, but second-rate scholarship. Would professor Sproul allow his students to make such bold assertions without credible citation?

[53]For a detailed refutation of this assertion, see Bente, *Historical Introduc-tions to the Book of Concord*, 209–28.

are a few places where double predestination, though never speci-
fied as such, seems to be supported by Luther, but as Bayer observes,
Luther uses a different form of speech than Calvin with respect to
predestination.[54] This has led eminent historical theologians, such as
Lewis Spitz and Alistair McGrath, to opposing conclusions regarding Luther's view, proving that nailing the reformer's position down
by isolating this book from the rest of his corpus is not as simple as
some would like to make it.[55]

It is also here that Luther begins to distinguish between God
hidden (*Deus absconditus*) and God revealed (*Deus revelatus*),
so that we read, "Wherever God hides himself, and wills to be
unknown to us, there we have no concern."[56] Luther consistently
maintained that we should not attempt to pry into the hidden will
of God; instead, we should concern ourselves solely with the self-
revelation of God in Christ Jesus as presented in Scripture. Luther's
reluctance toward a philosophic approach to theology, particularly
on questions regarding the will of God in election, is a matter in
which he grew more pastoral and cautious as his thought matured.
Reformed dogmatician, Herman Bavinck (1854–1921), provides an
accurate assessment:

> Luther accordingly, increasingly avoided the speculative doctrine of
> predestination, the will of divine good pleasure, the hidden God, pre-
> ferring to focus on the ministry of Word and sacraments, to which
> grace is bound, and giving increasing prominence to God's universal
> redemptive will, his expressed will.[57]

Lastly, even if Sproul's claim concerning Luther was true—
which I vehemently deny—he (that is, Luther) is not the final authority for Lutherans when it comes to doctrine. He is certainly revered
as a blessed father in the faith, but we recognize (just as he did) that
he is a sinner justified by faith for the sake of Christ, and therefore,

---

[54]Bayer, *Martin Luther's Theology*, 208.

[55]Spitz, *Renaissance and Reformation*, 2:420; McGrath, *Iustitia Dei*, 15–16.

[56]Luther, *Bondage of the Will*, 170.

[57]Bavinck, *Reformed Dogmatics*, 2:356.

fallible. For Lutherans, the sole rule and norm by which all doctrines and teachers are evaluated and judged are the Old and New Testaments alone.[58]

Now that both sides of the debate have been summarized and common caricatures cleared, we are ready to address the so-called *locus classicus* of Romans 9:6–24 that allegedly provides biblical proof for the Reformed doctrine of reprobation.[59]

A Merciful God: Setting Romans 9–11 in Context

It is well known that Paul wrote with a level of doctrinal depth and breadth that proved difficult for his readers—both then and now. Peter acknowledged as much when he wrote, "Some things in these [Paul's] letters are hard to understand, things the ignorant and unstable twist to their own destruction, as they also do to the rest of the Scriptures" (2 Pet 3:16). Perhaps he had Romans 9–11 in mind?

Here Paul builds upon an argument he began in the second chapter concerning the relationship between Jews and Gentiles, Law and Gospel, and the impartiality of God's salvation for all with the advent of the Messiah. The Jew can no longer appeal to a moral superiority based on his performance or possession of the Law (2:1–16); nor can he rest upon national privilege (2:17–24) or the rite of circumcision (2:25–29) in order to stand justified before God.

Does this mean that all the advantages Israel possessed were to no avail? "No, of course not," says Paul. They were entrusted with the "promises of God" (3:2); to them belongs the adoption as sons, the glory, the covenants, the law, temple, the promises and the patriarchs (9:4). The culminating privilege of Israel is that "to them belongs the Christ according to his natural descent."[60] The tragic and unexpected irony in the story is that Israel rejected her Messiah, whereas many Gentiles have come to faith.

---

[58]Formula of Concord, Epitome Summary, 1, *Triglotta*, 777.

[59]Baugh, "God's Purpose According to Election," 5: "And though there are many places where predestination is explicitly or implicitly taught, it is most clearly and definitively taught in chapter nine of Paul's Epistle to the Romans."

[60]Matthew stresses this point by tracing Jesus' ancestry to the beginning (Matt 1:1–17).

It is this question of God's faithfulness to His covenant promises that chiefly occupies Paul in chapters 9–11 as he enlists an imaginary Jewish interlocutor in order to absolve God of the charges of being unfaithful and unjust. Far from being a treatise on the doctrine of election and reprobation, this passage provides a historical overview of how God has sovereignly been at work within the lives of the patriarchs, prophets, and nations to bring the promised Savior, "who is God over all, blessed forever!" (9:5). This should come as no surprise as Paul is simply employing the hermeneutic that Jesus taught, "Beginning with Moses and all the Prophets, he explained to them what was said in all the Scriptures concerning himself" (Luke 24:27).

Following a touching display of angst and tension over his fellow Jews (9:1–5), Paul advances his argument in three distinct phases of Israel's story: (1) Israel in the past (9:6–29); (2) Israel in the present (9:30–10:21); and (3) Israel in the future (11:1–36).[61]

Question 1: Has the Word of God Failed? (Rom 9:6)

It is not as though the word of God had failed. For not all those who are descended from Israel are truly Israel . . .

God has not broken his promise! Paul makes it clear that being a Jew does not *de facto* make you a child of the Abrahamic promise, something he has already stressed in this letter. "For this reason by faith so that it may be by grace, with the result that the promise may be certain to all the descendants—not only to those who are under the law, but also to those have the faith of Abraham, who is the father of us all" (Rom 4:16).

Abraham is not simply the father of *physical* Israel as he is also the father of *spiritual* Israel—including Gentiles—who have now been grafted in and justified for the sake of Christ. Paul writes in a parallel passage, "And if you belong to Christ, then you are Abraham's descendants, heirs according to promise" (Gal 3:29).

Throughout Romans Paul has maintained that the Gospel reveals "the righteousness of God" (1:17), including the fact that God is true to his Word. "Let God be true and every man a liar" (3:4).

---

[61]Tobin, *Paul's Rhetoric in its Context*, 321.

Thus, verse 9:6 is the key to unlock how chapters 9–11 relate to the overall thesis of the letter.[62] In order to defend the "righteousness of God" thesis, Paul must break what Jonathan Grothe calls the "physical descent" hermeneutic of his Jewish naysayers, so he provides two patriarchal examples from Israel's history to do just that.[63]

Example 1: Isaac vs. Ishmael (Rom 9:7–9)

[7]*nor are all the children Abraham's true descendants; rather "through Isaac will your descendants be counted."* [8]*This means it is not the children of the flesh who are the children of God; rather, the children of promise are counted as descendants.* [9]*For this is what the promise declared: "About a year from now I will return and Sarah will have a son."*

God called and made covenant promises to Abraham and Sarah to bless all people on earth through their descendants (Gen 12:1–3). But the years passed and Sarah remained barren. Rather than wait upon the Lord and trust his word, Sarah took matters into her own hands by encouraging Abraham to bed her maidservant Hagar to produce an heir, which he did (Gen 16). But the son Ishmael born to the slave woman was not the son God promised.[64] Eventually, Sarah did miraculously bear a son in her old age according to promise. While both of Abraham's sons were children according to the flesh, only Isaac was the promised covenant heir.

This vignette of redemptive history clearly vindicates Paul's claim that God's promises are trustworthy. God established an everlasting covenant with Isaac and his descendants just as he had promised (Gen 17:19). This did not mean, however, that God treated Ishmael without mercy. God also blessed him and his descendants as he promised (Gen 17:20), though the Messiah would not come from his lineage. Once more Paul's goal is to break the "physical decent" hermeneutic of the Jews regarding the Messiah. Isaac displays how

---

[62]There is unanimity on this point between the majority of Reformed and Lutheran New Testament commentators.

[63]Grothe, *Justification of the Ungodly*, 2:476.

[64]See Galatians 4:22–26 for Paul's parallel use of this story.

God's choice of a covenant heir was dependent not on Abraham or Sarah, but upon the Lord's choice, timing, and provision.

Example 2: Jacob vs. Esau (Rom 9:10-13)

[10]*Not only that, but when Rebekah had conceived children by one man, our ancestor Isaac-*[11]*even before they were born or had done anything good or bad (so that God's purpose in election would stand, not by works but by his calling)-*[12]*it was said to her, "The older will serve the younger,"* [13]*just as it is written: "Jacob I loved, but Esau I hated."*

Paul's opponent could have reasoned that the example of Isaac was a weak one; after all, he was the natural born child of Sarah and not her Egyptian servant Hagar. But the twins Jacob and Esau shared the same womb. Additionally, Esau was the first born and by the law of primogeniture should have received Isaac's blessing to be the *paterfamilias* of the covenant family. But Paul takes it a step further and reminds his readers that God made this decision to favor Jacob "before they were born or had done anything good or bad." Why? So that God's "purpose in election would stand, not by works but by his calling" (9:11).

The first interpretive question at hand is whether or not the selection of Jacob over Esau pertains to a choice of eternal salvation or through which of them the Messiah would come. Sproul follows Calvin, as do most Reformed commentators, in preference of the former—the eternal election of the individual Jacob to salvation with Esau playing the part of the reprobate.[65] Such an interpretation does injustice to the immediate context of the passage as well as to the actual Old Testament narrative in order to squeeze into the text a Reformed doctrine of election that is foreign to Paul's train of thought.

The purpose clause concerning God's election and calling is linked directly to the quotation of Genesis 25:23 that immediately follows—the saying which Rebekah had received from God (i.e. the older will serve the younger). Despite birth order and the fact that he was an opportunistic deceiver, Jacob was selected and called to be

---

[65]Sproul, *Romans*, 314. See also, Calvin, *Commentaries*, 19:349.

a blessing to the nations through whom the Savior would come, the long awaited Seed of the woman promised to his grandfather Abraham (Gen 12:2–3). Yahweh's prophecy to Rebekah in Genesis 25:23 demonstrates that God's decision was not influenced by earthly circumstance (not by works but from the one who calls). Thus, charging God with unfaithfulness will not stand for he has kept his promise to extend the blessing through Abraham's descendants, though by default, it would not include all his children (i.e. Ishmael and Esau).

The second interpretive question is whether or not Paul utilizes Jacob and Esau only as "individuals" or as covenant heads of their respective "nations," or both. To answer this we must consider the second Old Testament reference, "Jacob I loved, but Esau I hated" (Mal 1:2–3). Sproul believes all references are attributed to them as individuals alone, and furthermore, states that any argument that suggests otherwise falls by its own weight. So confident is he with this verdict, that he concludes he does not know any serious New Testament scholar to advocate a differing opinion.[66]

I believe Sproul is too quick to dismiss the weight of Paul's Old Testament citations, for both speak of Jacob and Esau not only as individual men, but as representative men from whence come the nations of Israel and Edom. It is true that Paul only provides the last line of the oracle given to Rebekah, which implies the emphasis is on the two as individuals, but when the whole verse is read it gives us a more thorough understanding of why Paul found it only natural to include the prophet Malachi to support his argument: "*Two nations* are in your womb, and *two peoples* will be separated from within you. One people will be stronger than the other, and the older will serve the younger" (Gen 25:23, italics mine).

It is more than obvious that the prophetic message to Rebekah is not limited to her two sons. It demonstrates that God's sovereign plan expands well beyond the individual lives of Jacob and Esau to include their descendants—Israel and Edom (i.e. the two nations in her womb).

Paul's use of Malachi confirms God's fidelity to his promise as history corroborates the older did, in fact, serve the younger. The quote

---

[66]Sproul, *Romans*, 314.

in Malachi is not about *why* God chose one and not the other, but the *result* of that choosing.[67] As the centuries passed, the two nations became bitter enemies. Edom even participated in Israel's downfall (cf. Obad 10–14). While the passage is used by Paul to defend God's freedom and covenant fidelity toward Jacob and Israel, we find that Esau and Edom are judged and held responsible for their sin. There is absolutely no textual reason to force an either/or interpretation concerning Jacob and Esau; but rather, a both/and approach is more faithful to the entirety of the passages at play.

The last interpretive question we must ask concerns the meaning of the terms "love" and "hate" in the phrase, "Jacob I loved, but Esau I hated." Grothe is correct that neither in Malachi nor in Romans do the words mean that, according to God's free election in his eternal plan, only and all of the physical descendants of Jacob get to heaven and all the physical descendants of Esau go to hell.[68] Both terms have their meaning in relation to redemptive history, and not absolutely, as regards eternity. "Love" and "hate" are not emotions that God feels but respective actions he carries out in time. Hatred is better understood here to mean "not selected." The story of Jacob and the relationship to his wives, Leah and Rachel, provides further help regarding this love/hate dichotomy in Genesis 29:30–31, "So Jacob went in to Rachel also, and he loved Rachel more than Leah, and served Laban for another seven years. When the LORD saw that Leah was hated, he opened her womb, but Rachel was barren." Rachel was clearly favored by Jacob, but he stayed married to Leah and fathered six sons with her. Thus, the term "hated" should not be understood in the sense of contemporary English, but to mean "loved less."

C.E.B. Cranfield's observation regarding Esau merits inclusion for our present discussion concerning reprobation. "As in the case of Ishmael, so also with Esau, the rejected one is still, according to the testimony of Scripture, an object of God's merciful care."[69] The brothers eventually reconciled and together buried their father (Gen 33:29). God later reminds Israel, "You must not abhor an Edomite,

---

[67]Moldstad, "The Inspired Paradigm," 24.

[68]Grothe, *Justification of the Ungodly*, 2:468–69.

[69]Cranfield, *Romans*, 231.

for he is your brother" (Deut 23:7). Jacob was chosen to be the pro-
genitor of Israel and the Messiah, but the text gives no evidence that
Esau was eternally damned as a reprobate. Even Reformed scholar,
Douglas Moo, concedes that the Old Testament verses Paul cites do
not clearly refer to the eternal destiny of the individuals concerned.[70]

Paul is using the patriarchal narratives to demonstrate that God's
purpose has been accomplished in time (according to his choice and
by his call), in order to bring his Jewish brethren to repentance concerning the Messiah, proving that God's Word had not failed. Thus,
William Dumbrell adds, "But while God's conduct of the history
of salvation is the issue to which Paul is drawing our attention, the
issue of predestination, though implied, is not discussed nor is it in
view."[71] Paul is simply tracing the history of the Messianic promise.

Question 2: Is God Unjust? (Rom 9:14)

[14]*What shall we say then? Is there injustice with God? Absolutely not!*

As Paul breaks down the physical descent hermeneutic of Israel, he
anticipates the next accusation. If God's mercy is indiscriminate and
he has sovereignly moved history according to his own purpose with
no regard for ethnicity or good works, how can he still find fault? Is
God unjust or unrighteous? By no means![72] The problem with ques-
tioning the righteousness of God is that it judges God by human
standards. Paul rebuts the very suggestion by introducing the attribute of mercy as the character of God's action towards humanity; for
mercy, by its very nature, cannot be claimed or earned.[73]

To demonstrate once more that God is free to accomplish the
plan of salvation according to his own purpose, Paul introduces two
more examples from the next chapter of Israel's story—Moses and
Pharaoh.

---

[70]Moo, *Romans*, 571.

[71]Dumbrell, *Romans*, 100.

[72]See Romans 3:5 for a parallel. Nygren states that Paul does not merely
answer the question with a negative; he denies the propriety of even framing
the question in the first place, *Romans*, 365.

[73]Byrne, *Reckoning with Romans*, 189.

Example 1: Moses (Rom 9:15–16)

[15]*For he says to Moses: "I will have mercy on whom I will have mercy, and I will have compassion on whom I have compassion."* [16]*So then, it does not depend on human desire or exertion, but on God who shows mercy.*

Paul responds to the accusation by quoting Exodus 33:19 from the Septuagint. The background and context of the dialogue between God and Moses is vital and should not be ignored. Following the idolatrous golden calf affair at Mt. Sinai, God is determined to destroy Israel and start over (Exod 32:10). Like an ancient lawyer, Moses mounts a defense on Israel's behalf. It is interesting and relevant to our passage that God is unmoved by Moses' first attempt to sway him with the suggestion that he will be viewed as fickle and unjust by other nations (Exod 32:12). It is only when Moses appeals to God's covenant promises that he relents:

> Remember Abraham, Isaac, and Israel your servants, to whom you swore by yourself and told them, 'I will multiply your descendants like the stars of heaven, and all this land that I have spoken about I will give to your descendants, and they will inherit it forever' (Exod 32:13).

In desperate need of reassurance, Moses continues his advocacy work by asking to see the glory of God's abiding presence. Moses is ultimately granted this favor by seeing the glory of God's backside, and it is here that God proclaims, "I will have mercy on whom I will have mercy, and I will have compassion on whom I will have compassion."

The emphatic double repetition (*eleeso, oiktireso*) emphasizes the *sola gratia* of God's mercy. In parallel with 9:11, God's mercy is indiscriminate and independent of our desire or works. Paul is simply reminding his readers that it was for the sake of keeping his Word of promise to Abraham, Isaac, and Jacob that he showed mercy. Paul is again defending his main thesis of 9:6 that God's Word has not failed.

Example 2: Pharaoh (Rom 9:17–18)

[17]*For the scripture says to Pharaoh: "For this very purpose I have raised you up, that I may demonstrate my power in you, and that my name may be proclaimed in all the earth.* [18]*So then, God has mercy on whom he chooses to have mercy, and he hardens whom he chooses to harden."*

The divine purpose of raising Pharaoh to Egypt's throne is not mere omnipotence set over against mercy, but omnipotence serving mercy.[74] God's demonstration of power resulted in the rescue of Israel from bondage to Egypt in fulfillment of the promise made to Abraham (Gen 15:13–14). Paul is making use of another well-known example of Israel's past to illustrate how God has providentially moved redemptive history forward to fulfill His merciful covenant promises by quoting from Exodus 9:16. The word Paul employs for "raised up" (*exegeira*) is used in the LXX for calling up the actors on the stage of history for a particular purpose.[75]

> Everything in Genesis since the sale of Joseph to Egypt-bound Midianites has been happening in order to lead up to God's mighty salvation by the blood of the Lamb—the Passover and the Exodus, which point forward to the fulfillment in Jesus. The rise of a "Pharaoh who knew not Joseph" (Exod 1:8) was not just Egyptian politics-as-usual, but was God's seeing to it that a new ruler would enslave the Israelites and fill the role (in this salvation-historical drama) of "God's enemy" so that God would reveal his power.[76]

Reformed commentators hold up Pharaoh as the reprobate par excellence. Calvin speaks of the "predestination of Pharaoh to ruin."[77] Frame takes it even further as he makes the inference that runs from Pharaoh to unbelieving Israel, and by proxy, to all unbelievers.

> So, why is it that so many Israelites have not believed? Paul's answer, ultimately, is reprobation. Many Israelites have not believed because God sovereignly determined to prepare them for destruction, as he prepared others for glory.[78]

The problem with making such an interpretive leap is that there is no mention of predestination or reprobation in this example.

---

[74]Lenski, *Romans*, 614.

[75]Rogers and Rogers, *Exegetical Key to the Greek New Testament*, 333.

[76]Grothe, *Justification of the Ungodly*, 2:473.

[77]Calvin, *Commentaries*, 19:359.

[78]Frame, *Salvation Belongs to the Lord*, 181.

When the sequence of events leading to Pharaoh's hardening is actually taken into consideration, we find that out of twenty times prior to Exodus 9:16, ten speak of Pharaoh actively hardening his own heart in active rebellion against God's Word. It is not until the sixth plague of boils that we read for the first time, "But the Lord hardened Pharaoh's heart, and he did not listen to them, just as the Lord had predicted to Moses" (Exod 9:12). Despite being given numerous opportunities to relent and repent, Pharaoh continued to harden his heart and the Lord finally gave him over to his sinful choices (cf. Rom 1:24–28).

> But that God hardened Pharaoh's heart, namely, that Pharaoh always sinned again and again, and became the more obdurate, the more he was admonished, that was a punishment of his antecedent sin and horrible tyranny, which in many and manifold ways he practiced inhumanly and against the accusations of his heart toward the children of Israel.[79]

Many Calvinists fail to note this nuance in order to uphold God's sovereignty in their ongoing theological battle with synergists of varying stripes, but in doing so they miss how Pharaoh serves as an example of God's mercy. The key-word for Romans 9–11 is mercy, not sovereignty. Thus, I take issue with Moo's assertion that God raised up Pharaoh with a negative rather than positive purpose.[80] Pharaoh's hardening allowed for God's power and mercy to bless Israel. The Lord used the evil of Pharaoh ultimately for the good of his people who had been called according to his purpose (cf. Rom 8:28). We read nothing of a divine decree before the foundation of the world where God chose Pharaoh to have a hardened heart. Reading double predestination into this passage is textbook eisegesis. The story of Pharaoh is better placed under the *locus* of providence, and not election.

Before moving on to Paul's last rhetorical question, there are two aspects of obduracy (hardening) that should be mentioned. Horton acknowledges the first. "God is not active in hardening hearts in the

---

[79]Formula of Concord, Solid Declaration, XI, 85, *Triglotta*, 1091.
[80]Moo, *Romans*, 595.

same way that he is active in softening hearts."[81] Paul has already reminded his readers of humanity's level playing field when it comes to God. Everyone is a sinner deserving of death and judgment (Rom 3:10–20). Reformed and Lutheran stand together on this matter, "If any individual is to be saved, it must be by mercy only, and mercy falls into an entirely different category from justice."[82]

Secondly, God's hardening does not mean that it is arbitrary or always final. When we turn to Romans 11:11, Paul queries, "I ask then, they did not stumble into an irrevocable fall, did they? Absolutely not! But by their transgression salvation has come to the Gentiles, to make Israel jealous." Israel's hardening serves the purpose of expanding God's kingdom with the inclusion of the Gentiles, but all is not lost for Israel. Paul holds out hope for his fellow countrymen. He looks ahead to a time when Israel, numbering a great multitude, will come to believe in Christ. Paul says in the very next verse, "Now if their transgression means riches for the world and their defeat means riches for the Gentiles, how much more will their full restoration bring?" (11:12).

Question 3: Why Does He Still Find Fault? (Rom 9:19-21)

[19]*You will say to me then, "Why does he still find fault? For who has ever resisted his will? [20]But who indeed are you—a mere human being—to talk back to God? Does what is molded say to the molder, "Why have you made me like this?" [21]Has the potter no right to make from the same lump of clay one vessel for special use and another for ordinary use?*

Paul anticipates a natural objection with this final question. When one attempts to scale the height of God's absolute freedom, it arouses a sense of injustice. If God's mercy cannot be apprehended by physical descent, good works, or sheer willpower, then how can he still find fault? If salvation ultimately rests in God's merciful hand, reason revolts by shifting the blame back to God.

---

[81]Horton, *Christian Faith*, 317.

[82]Boice and Ryken, *Doctrines of Grace*, 107.

Such questions inevitably lead one into the philosophical shoal waters of God's freedom and human responsibility, but Paul will not allow himself to be run aground by such complaints for the person making them forgets they are a creature. And a creature does not have the right to talk back to his creator. Thus, Paul brings his interlocutor back down to earth by drawing upon the common Old Testament metaphor of the potter and clay.

> Your thinking is perverse! Should the potter be regarded as clay? Should the thing made say about its maker, "He didn't make me" or should the pottery say about the potter, "He doesn't understand?" (Is 29:16; so also 45:9).

Dumbrell's caution is noteworthy as we must not push the metaphor beyond its intended purpose:

> God's sovereignty is not arbitrary but serves his purpose of mercy (v. 23). This is not an abstract discussion of determinism or election. Paul is speaking nationally of Israel here, and is indicating the 'potter' analogy that God chose Israel in the first place, and thus has the right to remake her if she fails or does not conform to his standards (vv. 21–22, cf. Jer 18:1–6). Thus, though we might not be able to see it, there is ultimate consistency and unity in the display of God's character. His plan to move to the ends he has in view demands the historical choices made.[83]

God has been moving history forward by making choices, calling specific people or nations to particular roles—Isaac over Ishmael, Jacob over Esau, Pharaoh to display his power and Israel to receive mercy—all leading to his choice of a unwed virgin who would birth Israel's Messiah.

When Paul speaks of the potter fashioning two vessels out of the same lump of clay, both vessels serve a purpose.[84] In the context of this chapter, Paul uses both vessels—Moses and Pharaoh,

---

[83]Dumbrell, *Romans*, 101.

[84]For parallels, see Wisdom 15:7 and 2 Timothy 2:10.

unbelieving Israelites and believing Gentiles—to demonstrate that God had not forgotten his promise.

Objects of Wrath (Rom 9:22)

[22]*But what if God, willing to demonstrate his wrath and make known his power, has endured with much patience the objects of wrath prepared for destruction?*

While Paul is still responding to the objection of verse 19, he is drawing the overall thesis of 9:6 to a close. Verses 22–23 present a grammatical challenge for translators as they form an incomplete sentence. Paul begins with the protasis of a conditional sentence (*If God . . .*), leaving the apodosis to be supplied by the reader. Differences of interpretation largely rest on how the adverbial participle, "willing" (*thelon*), is to be translated and thus interpreted. Some translate the participle as causal: "choosing" (NIV) or "desiring" (ESV). The impression of a causal translation leads one to believe that God is patiently putting up with the vessels of wrath because he has actively chosen them to show his wrath and display his power. Reformed commentators like Moo argue that God's patience is serving the cause of his wrath, but as I have shown, the entire thrust of the chapter has been to uphold God's mercy and word of promise. Thus, the participle is best understood concessively, translating it, "although willing." In other words, God has willingly endured Israel's rejection of the gospel to demonstrate his wrath—that is, to show what happens to people when they reject his mercy in Christ Jesus. The objects of wrath receive nothing more than they have chosen.

Furthermore, in keeping with our first hermeneutical principle of interpreting Scripture with Scripture, we find this line of reasoning consistent with what Paul has stated earlier in the letter, "But because of your stubbornness and your unrepentant heart, you are storing up wrath for yourselves in the day of wrath, when God's righteous judgment is revealed" (Rom 2:5).

We gain further clarity when we grasp the manner in which Paul describes the state of such unbelief. They are "prepared for destruction" (*katertismena*). The English verb "prepared" lacks the nuance of the Greek, and if we are not careful, it can lead one to the conclusion that God is the one who has actively prepared or formed these vessels for destruction. If the participle is viewed as a passive, as most Calvinists insist, it is argued that God is the active subject who made them for such a purpose. Thus, Calvin speaks of the vessels of wrath as those "made and formed for this end, that they may be examples of God's vengeance and displeasure."[85] Such a reading goes well beyond God merely "passing over the reprobate and leaving them to their own devices," as Sproul repeatedly emphasizes.[86] But more importantly, it disregards the fact that God does not desire the death of the wicked, but rather they turn and live (Ezek 18:23).

The participle can also be interpreted in the middle voice, which would lead us to conclude that the objects of wrath had "prepared themselves for . . ." or "were in a state of ripeness."[87] Reformed commentator, William Hendriksen, admits that the participle Paul uses does not state who it was that prepared these people or made them ripe for destruction.[88] This is because *katertismena* is a perfect participle, which does not emphasize the action of the verb, but its state or condition.

The interpretation the Lutheran confessors settled upon is the most faithful to the text:

> Here, then, the apostle clearly says that God endured with long suffering the vessels of wrath, but does not say that He made them vessels of wrath; for if this had been His will, He would not have required any great long suffering for it. The fault, however, that they are fitted for destruction belongs to the devil and to men themselves, and not to God.[89]

Even though the objects of wrath deserve destruction, and God is willing to grant such an end, he is long suffering in his patience toward them. This suggests that God is patiently waiting for their repentance. It is certainly congruous with Peter's understanding of

---

[85]Calvin, *Commentaries*, 19:368.

[86]Sproul, *What is Reformed Theology?*, 159.

[87]So argues Lenski, *Romans*, 622.

[88]Hendricksen, *Romans*, 328.

[89]Formula of Concord Solid Declaration, XI, 80, *Triglotta*, 1089.

God's patience as it relates to God's Word of promise, "The Lord is not slow concerning his promise, as some regard slowness, but is being patient toward you, because he does not wish for any to perish but for all to come to repentance" (2 Pet 3:9). Lastly, Paul does not give any credence to the notion that the objects of wrath are forever consigned to such a role from eternity (i.e. reprobate).

Objects of Mercy (Rom 9:23–24)

[23]And what if he is willing to make known the wealth of his glory on the objects of mercy that he has prepared beforehand for glory—[24]even us, whom he has called, not only from the Jews but also from the Gentiles?

Paul describes the vessels of mercy differently than the vessels of wrath in the previous verse. In order to make known the wealth of his mercy, God has "prepared beforehand" (NET, ESV) or "prepared in advance" (NIV) the objects of mercy for glory. Here Paul makes use of an active verb (*proetoimasen*).[90] The prefix *pro-* denotes God preparing those who receive mercy in advance or ahead of time. We do here at last find a possible reference to God's election, and the differing verbal forms Paul uses to distinguish the two vessels serves to uphold the single predestination view.

The apostle reveals the identity of those for whom God will make known the "wealth of his glory" in verse 24. I quote Grothe's summary at length as he captures the heart of Paul's thought:

> Since one becomes such a "vessel of mercy" by God's call rather than by virtue of physical birth, then the Word of God can call and create such vessels, as God wills, freely, from among both Jews and Gentiles—even as he was free to select (and did select) Isaac instead of Ishmael, Jacob instead of Esau, for the historical favor of bearing the promise of the Seed. A corollary is that it is "some" "from" (*ek*) both the Jews and the Gentiles who are now ones whom "God called." Jews are not automatically included by birth as Jews. Both the inclusion of some Gentiles and the exclusion of some Jews is testified in

---

[90]The only other use of the compound verb, *proetoimasen*, occurs in Ephesians 2:10 where Paul speaks of "the good works which God prepared beforehand."

the OT Scripture, as the following quotations attest, supporting the hermeneutical principle from which Paul departed (9:6–8) and at which his argument has arrived (9:24).[91]

Make Mine a Single

Michael Horton concludes:

> The hidden God is not different from the revealed God. All of the elect will be saved, without the possibility of one being lost. At the same time, the well-meant summons of the external Word to repent and believe the gospel is universal. That many do in fact embrace Christ is a miracle of God's electing grace, realized in history.[92]

I could not agree more, but what of the many who do not embrace Christ? Does God stand behind their persevering unbelief and ultimate rejection by virtue of an eternal decree as the Reformed church teaches? The Lutheran tradition answers in Pauline fashion, "By no means!"

The scriptures, including the ninth chapter of Romans, do not support an eternal decree of reprobation. To be sure, "God is just in leaving unbelievers in their ruin and fall into which they plunged themselves," as the Belgic Confession states, but the crux of the debate is centered on whether or not God consigned them to such an end before the foundation of the world. The entirety of Romans 9–11 centers on the "riddle of Israel" as Brunner puts it. God is free to reject Israel because of her unbelief without, therefore, becoming unfaithful to his promise.[93] As one continues to read through chapters 10 (Israel's present) and 11 (Israel's future), Paul never once holds God responsible for Israel's rejection; but rather, it is on account of her own rejection of God's righteousness found in Christ alone that unbelieving Israel finds herself a vessel of wrath, which the following summary outlines:

---

[91]Grothe, *Justification of the Ungodly*, 2:487.

[92]Horton, *Christian Faith*, 322.

[93]Brunner, *Romans*, 88–89.

- Israel pursued righteousness in Torah based upon works, rather than submitting to God's righteousness through faith in Christ (9:32–33; 10:3–4).
- The branches of unbelieving Israel were broken off because of their unbelief, the remnant of believing Jews stand by faith (11:20).
- God has granted a partial hardening on Israel until the full number of Gentiles has come to faith (11:25), thus affirming that God's hardening does not in every case bespeak reprobation or a finality of one's eternal destiny.
- Paul holds out hope for the unbelieving Jews who have been temporarily broken off in the present. "And even they [unbelieving Jews]—if they do not continue in their unbelief—will be grafted in, for God is able to graft them in again" (11:23).
- At present they are enemies of the Gospel and the Church, but "in regard to election they are dearly loved for the sake of the fathers. For the gifts and the call of God are irrevocable" (11:28–29). The very examples that Reformed theologians hold up as the chief examples of the *double decree* are "dearly loved" by God.

The Bible affirms that whoever is saved is so by God's grace alone; whoever is lost is so solely by his or her own fault. Sproul insists there are "elect" and "non-elect."[94] Lutherans affirm the same, but those who ultimately fall into the category of "non-elect" are so by their own accord, not by God's negative decree before the foundation of the world. Calvinism's "double or nothing" approach moves well beyond the bounds of Holy Scripture. I respond, "Make mine a single!"

---

[94]Sproul, *Truths We Confess*, 1:87.

The Sacramental Word

An Introduction to Sacramental Thought

Augustine's famous maxim of the sacraments as "visible words" of the gospel has formed the bedrock from which the entire Western sacramental tradition has been constructed. Therefore, it should come as no surprise that Wittenberg and Geneva share an Augustinian lexicon when it comes to the sacraments by making manifold use of words like sign, seal, pledge, and means of grace. Sproul observes that churches have historically understood the sacraments in vastly different ways, but because they are so important to the life of the church, it is understandable that there has been a lot of controversy.[95] The difficulty when comparing our traditions is compounded by the fact that neither side defines or applies our inherited sacramental vocabulary in the same way. The result has led to confusion and mischaracterization, adding to the controversies of which Sproul speaks; and often, we have simply found ourselves talking past one another, using the same words, but meaning different things by them. To alleviate some of the confusion, as well as highlight specific areas of disagreement, I have included an excursus on the sacraments in general before treating Baptism and the Lord's Supper in the chapters that follow. This chapter is especially written for those who may be unfamiliar with how Lutherans approach the Word of God.

---

[95]Sproul, *Truths We Confess*, 3:78.

The Forms of God's Efficacious Word

The term "sacrament" comes from the Latin, *sacramentum*, referring to something that has been consecrated.[96] While it is not a biblical term, it was adopted by Latin-speaking Christians from the time of Tertullian (AD 160–220) to denote those specific promise-bearing rites instituted by Jesus to be a public and perpetual means of grace for the furtherance of the gospel and the strengthening of his church. Lutherans and Calvinists recognize Baptism and the Lord's Supper as sacraments in contrast to the seven enumerated by the Church of Rome.[97] Lutherans further define the Church as the "the congregation of saints, in which the gospel is rightly taught and the sacraments are rightly administered," meaning the sacraments are an essential mark of the church.[98]

Luther said that God's Word cannot be without God's people and, conversely, God's people cannot be without God's Word.[99] To better understand Luther's teaching about Word and Sacrament, it is helpful to relate his theology of the Word to the incarnation of Jesus, and more specifically, to his theology of the cross:

> God has come to us in the crucified man Jesus. This is the theology of the Cross. But that crucified God is an offense to all our own expectations and ideas. Therefore, if we want to meet Him, we must leave our own wisdom and experience behind us and listen to that Word, which in God's name and against our reason declares the crucified man to be "God for us."[100]

---

[96]For a short history of this, and the related term, *mysterion*, as well as their development in sacramental thought from Augustine to Peter Lombard, see Cary, *Outward Signs*, 158–61.

[97]Lutherans also include Absolution in our Symbols (Apology XIII, 4), but because of its lack of a visible element, Luther connected it closely to Baptism (*Babylonian Captivity*, LW, 36:124). I would argue that the minister speaking on behalf of Christ, standing *in persona Christi*, is the visible sign of Absolution, but that is an argument for another time.

[98]Augsburg Confession, VII, *Triglotta*, 47. Reformed Confessions acknowledge the same, but add "discipline" as a third mark.

[99]Cited in Lull, *Basic Theological Writings*, 547.

[100]Prenter, *Martin Luther Lectures*, 2:66.

Where do we find this crucified man to be God for us? Luther's answer was in the external Word and Sacraments. Forgiveness was achieved by Christ on the cross, but it is not distributed there. Since we cannot go back in time to Calvary, the benefits of the crucified man must come to us through the means God has graciously provided.[101] The Word of God is living and active (Heb 4:12), and because it is God's Word, it always accomplishes that for which he sends it (Isa 55:11). Robert Kolb and Charles Arand summarize the efficacious nature of the Word:

> When the Holy Spirit fashions the message of Christ in human language, these words are God's Word and an effective expression of his power. They do what he wants them to do. God acts through the words that he calls "gospel" to do more than inform human beings about his own disposition toward them. His Word is what modern linguists call "performative speech." Indeed, it is "creative speech." It accomplishes his will and actualizes his presence in human lives.[102]

Long before J.L. Austin pioneered Speech Act theory for linguistic studies, Lutherans described God's Word as a "deed-word." God is the subject doing all the saving verbs through the means of his living Word. God is abundantly rich in his mercy and sends this efficacious Word in several forms:

1. The *oral* Word through preaching and absolution (Rom 10:14; John 20:23);
2. The *scriptural* Word of the Old and New Testaments (2 Tim 3:14–16); and, lastly,

---

[101]Luther spoke at length on this against Karlstadt and other "enthusiasts" who rejected the means of grace in favor of a spiritually subjective approach to God (*Against the Heavenly Prophets*, LW, 40:144–223).

[102]Kolb and Arand, *The Genius of Luther's Theology*, 135. Calvin also spoke of the Word as *verbum sacramentale*, a sacramental Word, *Institutes*, 4.14.4. Gerrish observes that Calvin felt no antagonism between what we may call the "pedagogical" (teaching) and the "sacramental" functions of the word, *Grace and Gratitude*, 84. We must keep in mind, however, that for Calvin, this is the preached Word.

3. The *sacramental* Word through Baptism, Absolution, and the Lord's Supper.[103]

Lutherans and Reformed have, by and large, stood on common ground when it comes to the significance of the oral and scriptural word, but on the sacramental word there remains an unfortunate divide.

Lutherans by no means set limitations on what God can do, but simply affirm that he has promised to work through these chosen instruments of grace, and we should not seek him elsewhere. On this matter, Lutherans fall squarely into the historic catholic tradition.[104] Preus states that Luther had no interest in quibbling about exceptions or the possibility that God might save someone without the sacraments. "The Word of God commands the church to use them for the salvation of men. That is enough."[105] The Formula adds, "And by this means, and in no other way, namely, through His holy Word, when men hear it preached or read it, and the holy sacraments when they are used according to His Word, God desires to call men to eternal salvation, draw them to Himself, and convert, regenerate, and sanctify them."[106]

Luther accepted the fact that God as our creator had no difficulty making use of his material creation, using ordinary elements—water, bread, and wine—to support his efficacious Word and confer his saving grace. For example, Lutheran theologian David Scaer observes that Luther found it only natural to draw a line from the water in creation through the water of the Red Sea to the water in baptism. In all these acts, God kills (buries) and makes alive (resurrects). God is working through coverings, that is, sacraments, to come to His people. All Old and New Testament rites are

---

[103]This division is also commonly used by Reformed scholars. For example, Godfrey speaks of the preached Word, written Word, incarnate Word (Jesus), and visible Word (sacraments), "Why Baptism?," 28.

[104]For more reasons, see Cary, "Why Luther is Not Quite Protestant," 447–86.

[105]Cited in Preus, *A Theology to Live By*, 146.

[106]Formula of Concord, Solid Declaration, II, 50, *Triglotta*, 901.

qualitatively the same kinds of divine actions in that God is working in and through them.[107]

Lutherans and Calvinists split over the sacraments in two primary ways: sacramental efficacy (the powerful effect of the sacraments) and sacramental presence (God manifest through these means). Each of these will be explored in-depth in the next three chapters, but for our purposes here, I will point out a few subordinate areas of thought that further contribute to the debate and our present disunity.

Sacramental Signs and Significance

Understanding the Bible's teaching on the sacraments would be much easier if we restricted ourselves to biblical terminology, but when dealing with the historical development of a doctrine, we must become acquainted with the technical terms and concepts of a given era. This is most certainly true of the sacraments. Following Augustine, the Reformers thought of the sacraments as "visible signs that signify spiritual realities." According to Augustine, the "signs" (*signum*) are material elements regarded not for what they are in themselves, but for their use in pointing to deeper, unseen realities. The Latin term Augustine used to denote what the sign signifies is *res*, the thing or reality. For example, the external *signum* of the Lord's Supper are bread and wine, while the internal *res* are Christ's body and blood. Calvin cites Augustine approvingly on this distinction.[108]

Luther's theology of sacramental efficacy, by way of contrast, originates within the framework of medieval sacramental thought. According to Philip Cary, "His teaching that the Gospel of Christ is a divine promise effectually giving the salvation it promises grows out of the medieval conception of sacramental signs effectually conferring the inward grace they signify."[109] When Luther thinks of the

---

[107]Scaer, "Reformed Exegesis and Lutheran Sacraments," 16.

[108]Calvin, *Institutes*, 4.14.15. When reading Calvin in English, we must keep in mind that when he says Christ's body is the "substance" of the sacrament, the Latin term he uses is *res*.

[109]Cary, *Outward Signs*, viii.

body and blood of Christ in the Supper, he associates them with the sacramental signs (*signum*), not just the thing they signify (*res*). Here Luther breaks with Augustine and more closely aligns with theologians like Peter Lombard (AD 1100–1160), while simultaneously denying the *opere operato* that had begun to develop during this period.[110]

Sacramental thought had shifted significantly in the early twelfth century, when Hugh of St. Victor (AD 1069–1140) altered Augustine's definition. For him the rite itself (*sacramentum tantum*) not only pointed to the inner reality (*res*), but also contained and conveyed that inner reality. This adjustment eventually assumed the sacramental standard by the increasingly widespread use of Lombard's *Sentences* as a primary theological textbook, which only confirmed the long held conviction that believers encountered the risen Lord *in* the sacramental rites.[111]

Calvin rejected Lombard's classification, and specifically denied that Christ's body can be spoken of as *sacramentum*.[112] Thus, when Calvin argues that external signs can have no intrinsic spiritual power, he is right to insist that Augustine is on his side. As Brian Gerrish observes, "It is hardly too much to say that Calvin's entire sacramental theology lies implicit in his doctrine of signs (which, of course, he borrowed from St. Augustine)."[113] Cary captures this distinction well:

> In one sense, of course, all of Western theology is Augustinian, including the matter of word and sacrament, both of which are conceived as outward signs of inner things. But the Augustinian framework assumes the superiority of the inner as well as the superficiality of the external, so it is striking when medieval theologians defend a piety that clings to external things and Luther follows them, while Calvin and subsequent tradition of Protestant inwardness spurn this kind

---

[110]For example, *Babylonian Captivity*, LW, 36:43–45.

[111]For this historical development, see Finn, "The Sacramental World in the Sentences of Peter Lombard," 557–82.

[112]Calvin, *Institutes*, 4.17.33.

[113]Gerrish, "John Calvin," 233.

of externalism. The fault line opens up in the twelfth century when medieval theologians first define sacraments as external signs that not only signify an inner grace but confer it. Calvin, unlike Luther, rejects this confidence in the efficacy of external things and looks back past medieval sacramental theology to its deeper roots in Augustine.[114]

There was no reason for Luther to look past the sacraments for deeper realities, because in them he found the promise and presence of God they signified.

The Spirit, Sacraments, and *Sola Fide*

The Reformed tradition is reluctant to accept that God can, and indeed does, work through external signs (*signum*) to bring sinners into saving union with Christ through the Holy Spirit. Scaer detects a neo-Platonic Augustinian bias when it comes to how Calvinists approach the Bible. Reformed exegetes consistently, though perhaps unknowingly, incorporate this philosophy into their biblical methodology, which, predictably, results in a minimalist sacramental hermeneutic, since the Spirit's immediate working obviates a saving necessity for the sacraments.[115]

Following Article IV in the Augsburg Confession concerning justification by faith alone, Article V extols the means by which God justifies sinners:

> To obtain such faith God instituted the office of preaching, giving the gospel and the sacraments. Through these, as through means, he gives the Holy Spirit who produces faith, where and when he wills, in those who hear the gospel. It teaches that we have a gracious God, not through our merit but through Christ's merit, when we so believe.[116]

Notice the relationship between the Word, Sacrament, and Holy Spirit. They are bound inseparably together and work in one

---

[114]Cary, *Outward Signs*, viii.

[115]Scaer, "Reformed Exegesis and Lutheran Sacraments," 9.

[116]Augsburg Confession, V, *Book of Concord* (Kolb-Wengert), 40

indissoluble act. The Spirit uses both the oral and sacramental forms of God's Word to justify sinners who receive the Gospel in faith.

When it comes to the sacraments, Lutherans do not divorce the visible sign from the Word. It is paramount that this be understood. Without the Word, there is no sacrament—only water, bread, and wine. To use Luther's formulation for Baptism in the Small Catechism, "Baptism is not simple water only, but it is the water *comprehended* in God's command and *connected* with God's Word."[117] For a sacrament to be a true sacrament, Chemnitz says, two things are necessary:

1. The express and universal command of God, covering the universal church of the New Testament, regarding some external or visible element or sure sign and a prescribed rite for administration and use.
2. The promise of the Gospel regarding the free mercy of God for the sake of Christ added to this rite in the Word in such a way that through it this [mercy] is offered, shown, applied, and sealed to individuals who use the sacraments in true faith.[118]

Lutherans reject the Roman Catholic notion that the sacraments work automatically (*ex opera operato*). Neither do we attribute efficacy to the visible element or to the one administering it. This we share with our Reformed brethren as confirmed by the Westminster Confession:

> The grace which is exhibited in or by the sacraments rightly used, is not conferred by any power in them; neither does the efficacy of a sacrament depend upon the piety or intention of him that does administer it: but upon the work of the Spirit, and the word of institution, which contains, together with a precept authorizing the use thereof, a promise of benefit to worthy receivers.[119]

---

[117]Small Catechism, IV, 1, *Triglotta*. 551, emphasis mine. This is consistent with Augustine's statement, "Let the word be added to the element and it will become a sacrament," in which Calvin also agrees, *Institutes*, 4.14.4.

[118]Chemnitz, *Loci Theologica*, 2:724.

[119]Westminster Confession, XXVII, 3.

The Westminster divines sought to safeguard the sacraments from sacerdotalism, which is admirable; yet in his commentary on the Westminster Confession, Sproul argues that the Protestant doctrine of justification by faith alone implies that the sacraments do not have the power to save. They are important, according to Sproul, but they do not confer salvation.[120] Horton likewise writes, "Baptism does not cause any one of the links in the chain of personal salvation (including regeneration) to occur; rather it ratifies God's pledge to apply all of the benefits of salvation. It is a sign and seal of the covenant of grace."[121] Sproul and Horton depreciate the sacraments, in my opinion, by tearing the Spirit asunder from the sacramental Word. Faith is always presupposed in their confessions and catechisms, thus Baptism is downgraded from being an instrument of the Spirit's regenerative work, losing its disciple making significance for which Christ commissioned it (Matt 28:19). Baptism can encourage the faithful, according to Calvin, by providing a covenantal stamp of approval, but it cannot bring the covenant relationship into being by actually uniting us to Christ's death and resurrection as Paul asserts (Rom 6:3–11). Jan Rohls' assessment is accurate, "For the Reformed these rites are means of grace only in a noetic sense—to inform us that God gives grace—but not in the rites themselves."[122]

Presbyterian scholar, Murray, confirms this in his understanding of sacramental efficacy by following the Westminster Directory for Public Worship:

> Since they are signs and seals, they presuppose the existence of the blessings they represent, and therefore are not to be conceived of as the means of establishing or constituting the relationship signified. Hence the grace symbolized is conveyed apart from their use. They are not themselves the means of salvation, or of the union with Christ by which the state of salvation is effected.[123]

---

[120]Sproul, *Truths We Confess*, 3:90.

[121]Horton, "Union and Communion," 406, citing Westminster Confession, XXVIII, 1 for further support.

[122]Rohls, *Reformed Confessions*, 185–86.

[123]Murray, *Collected Works*, 2:367.

The sacraments represent God's grace, but by no measure will Murray admit that they are the Spirit's means for creating and sustaining faith. God is condescending to his creatures by using visible signs, like a children's object lesson teaching us about God's grace, but the recipient of the sacrament must turn elsewhere for actual grace, since it is "presupposed" or "conveyed apart from its use."

Spiritus Sanctus: The Lord and Giver of Life

Sproul believes that the efficacy of a sacrament depends upon the work of the Spirit. He writes, "The Holy Spirit is the efficient cause of a person being cleansed of original sin and reborn."[124] But in the very next sentence, he denies that the Holy Spirit can use Baptism to bring this to pass, since such a belief would be inconsistent with the Reformers understanding of justification. He concludes, "The Protestant view, however, is that the instrumental cause of justification is faith. Faith is the instrument by which we lay hold of Christ, by whose righteousness we are redeemed."[125] Sproul's use of Luther is selective and misleading. In numerous works, he enlists Luther as a champion of Protestant orthodoxy, but on the sacraments and their relation to justification, Luther and his heirs stop being Protestant (and apparently, Luther is no longer counted among the Reformers).

Luther notes in his Small Catechism how one is actually called to saving faith by the Spirit:

> I believe that I cannot by my own reason or strength believe in Jesus Christ, my Lord, or come to Him; but the Holy Ghost has called me by the Gospel; enlightened me with His gifts, sanctified and kept me in the true faith; even as He calls, gathers, enlightens, and sanctifies the whole Christian Church on earth, and keeps it with Jesus Christ in the one true faith.[126]

In what way does the Holy Spirit come to us? According to Luther, the Holy Spirit engenders faith by means of the gospel. But

---

[124]Sproul, *Truths We Confess*, 3:92, 95.

[125]Sproul, *Truths We Confess*, 3:95.

[126]Small Catechism, II, 3, *Triglotta*, 545.

this gospel is a specific word that comes from another; it has the form of a word that can be heard, as well as seen and touched in the sacraments. The Spirit's call is bound together with baptism—"enlightened with His gifts." Bayer notes that its ongoing efficacy from cradle to grave is expressed by the use of the present perfect tense verbs in the catechism: "enlighten," "sanctify," and "preserve." The Holy Spirit does not do his work only when he brings justifying faith, but also works by the gift of faith to ensure the believer continues and remains in the one true faith.[127] In his *Confession Concerning Christ's Supper* (1528), Luther adds:

> But because this grace would benefit no one if it remained so profoundly hidden and could not come to us, the Holy Spirit comes and gives himself to us also, wholly and completely . . . He does this both inwardly and outwardly—inwardly by means of faith and other spiritual gifts, outwardly through the gospel, baptism, and the sacrament of the altar, through which as through three means or methods he comes to us and inculcates the sufferings of Christ for the benefit of our salvation.[128]

I appreciate Sproul's concern to protect *sola fide*, but faith must have something to cling to. The Holy Spirit does not bring faith apart from the outward means. Lutherans believe that God conveys salvation in and through the sacraments, because God has appointed them for this very purpose. To receive faith is to receive Christ and to receive Christ is to receive, by the work of the Holy Spirit, faith. The Spirit is doing the work to bring us to faith and justifies us for the sake of Christ, but He is doing so through the earthly elements comprehended by the Word. Thus, Paul can speak of Baptism as the "washing of the new birth and the renewing of the Holy Spirit, whom he poured out on us in full measure through Jesus Christ our Savior" (Titus 3:5–6).

While Reformed scholars treat the material elements of the sacraments as obstacles to God's transcendence, Lutherans see them as

---

[127]Bayer, *Martin Luther's Theology*, 241.

[128]Cited in Lull, *Basic Theological Writings*, 56.

complementary vehicles for his immanent saving actions that take place within our terrestrial reality. "Just as the Spirit brought creation to completion," Scaer writes, "so also he brings redemption to completion by creating faith through the created things he has designated for this purpose."[129]

The Outward Turn to an Embodied Word

By now, someone has likely asked, "Why all the fuss? Why do we even need the sacraments if they essentially do the same thing as the oral or scriptural Word?" Calvin answers:

> Here our merciful Lord, according to his infinite kindness, so tempers himself to our capacity that, since we are creatures who always creep on the ground, cleave to the flesh, and, do not think about or even conceive of anything spiritual, he condescends to lead us to himself even by these earthly elements, and to set before us in the flesh a mirror of spiritual blessings.[130]

Note the sharp dichotomy of earthly and spiritual. For Calvin, God is accommodating our lower, fleshly level by using earthly elements. He speaks of these elements as a condescension to our regrettable creeping, fleshly existence, since they provide for our creaturely weakness. The sacraments act as mirrors to reflect spiritual blessings, but the blessings are not contained therein. The trouble with such an answer is twofold.

First, Calvin gives preeminence to the oral Word. He places the sacraments in the soteriological back-seat by affording passages like Romans 10:17 (*faith comes by hearing*) greater theological weight over and above sacramental passages that speak of the same salvific blessings, such as Paul's autobiography in Acts 22:16 (*Get up, be baptized, and have your sins washed away*). Thus, Calvin can write, "You see how the sacrament requires preaching to beget faith."[131] But

---

[129]Scaer, "The Holy Spirit, Sacraments, and Church Rites," 317.

[130]Calvin, *Institutes*, 4.14.3.

[131]Calvin, *Institutes*, 4.14.4.

preaching is not beyond the realm of signs and our fleshly existence, for all utterances in language are audible signs that must be learned in order to comprehend the reality of the one speaking. Speaking and hearing require my body and mind to translate what is heard into meaning. There is, therefore, an externality even to the preached Word in that it is locatable and material, requiring fleshly things like a tongue, ears, and brain.

Preaching additionally makes us dependent on another to communicate the Gospel (*how are they to hear without someone preaching?*). External witnesses, such as Gospel preachers, are persons who are present for us in their flesh, and therefore, knowing other persons—including the Father, Son, and Holy Spirit—always takes place in an embodied way.

Words do more than simply inform. As speech act theorists have proven, words do things. For example, the vows spoken in a wedding ceremony change the bride and groom's relational identity. How much more so when these words are God's divine speech acts? The fact that this makes us dependent on what is outside us—a truth that comes to us only as a gift of the other—is the very goodness of it.[132]

Secondly, by following Augustine down into the rabbit hole of the inner self, as Calvin does, he paints an unnecessary, and frankly, unbiblical picture of humanity as he privileges unseen spiritual realities over visible creaturely realities.[133] Calvin says that it is because we have souls engrafted in bodies that God imparts spiritual things under visible ones.[134] But the body is not ancillary to our created being; we are a psychosomatic whole (body and soul), and therefore, true biblical anthropology must fight to keep humanity intact, lest we fall prey to the heresy of Gnosticism. Jesus did not atone for our souls alone, but for our entire created being, marking the necessity of the incarnation, "born of a woman, under the Law" (Gal 4:4), as well as the promise of bodily resurrection at Christ's return (1 Cor 15:12–21).

---

[132]Cary, *Outward Signs*, xiii.

[133]I am not using fleshly, creaturely, or bodily here in the sense of "the flesh" (*sarx*) as Paul does in Romans 7:5 to denote our sinful self (old Adam), but of humanity as enfleshed, material beings created by God.

[134]Calvin, *Institutes*, 4.14.3.

Robert Jenson illustrates the importance of bodily locatedness in communicating ourselves one to another, "My body is *myself*, in my address and presence to you, insofar as I am available to you, locatable by you, there for you, addressable in turn by you. And it is the visibility of my address to you that constitutes such reciprocity."[135] Whether the Gospel is spoken audibly or enacted visibly, Jenson concludes that it is Christ's self-presentation in our lives as the one risen and living person—spirit from one side and body from the other, as are all living persons—that he in fact is.[136] In other words, there is an external locatedness to Christ's promise and presence in the sacraments, and therefore, the Word is embodied.

Why are the sacraments so important? The answer lies in the relationship between the internal and external in the life of faith. Because we are sinners, we turn everything in upon ourselves (*curvatus in se*), thus, when left with the oral or written Word alone, we have a natural propensity towards internalizing the words. Sundered from the sacraments, we become prey, as Forde says, "to adverbial theology."[137] Do I really, sincerely, truly believe? As with Adam in the garden, the devil is adept at getting us to doubt God's Word, "Did God really say?" Sacraments save because they remain an external promise of God, and as Luther is always quick to remind, God does not lie (Rom 3:4). As Forde elaborates:

> They guarantee the character of the Word as what Luther could call an "alien" Word, a Word from without, from out there in the world of things and bodies . . . Sacraments save because they save the Word from disappearing into the inner life. They save because they prevent us from understanding grace as some kind of hidden agenda, a behind-the-scenes spiritualism that we are supposed somehow to master or learn the secret of . . . The devil, that master of subjectivity, can do nothing about the alien Word, the Word from without, the visible and tangible Word. It has simply happened and nothing can change that. As such it is part and parcel of the proclamation and must be preached against all objection . . . The fact that we are saved

---

[135]Jenson, *Dogmatics*, 2:304.

[136]Jenson, *Dogmatics*, 2:305.

[137]Forde, *Theology is for Proclamation*, 159.

by faith alone must not be taken to mean that we are saved by reliance on our own inner resources.[138]

One of the self-reliant "inner resources" we are saved from includes turning faith in upon itself. For example, Baptism prevents us from having what Cary calls a "reflective faith."[139] This inward turn is reinforced by the Reformed concept of "effectual calling." As Sproul defines it, this calling refers to the Holy Spirit's inward or secret operation on the soul.[140] For Lutherans, the doctrine of justification by faith alone does not mean we depend upon our faith. Faith is certainly a gift of God wrought by the Spirit, but it does not turn inward in search of a secret operation; rather, it relies on the truth of God's external and public promise accompanied by water, "I baptize you into the Name of the Father, and the Son, and the Holy Spirit." The object of faith, Jesus, is always an external and embodied reality. The incarnation, after all, did not end with his resurrection and ascension.

In his Large Catechism, Luther provides a very non-Protestant sounding response to those concerned with shielding *sola fide* from external things (like water in baptism):

> But as our would-be wise, new spirits assert that faith alone saves, and that works and external things avail nothing, we answer: It is true, indeed, that nothing in us is of any avail but faith, as we shall hear still further. But these blind guides are unwilling to see this, namely, that faith must have something which it believes, that is, of which it takes hold, and upon which it stands and rests. Thus faith clings to the water, and believes that it is Baptism, in which there is pure salvation and life; not through the water (as we have sufficiently stated), but through the fact that it is embodied in the Word and institution of God, and the name of God inheres in it. Now, if I believe this, what else is it than believing in God as in Him who has given and planted His Word into this ordinance, and proposes to us this external thing wherein we may apprehend such a treasure?[141]

---

[138]Forde, *Theology is for Proclamation*, 160–161.

[139]Cary, "Sola Fide: Luther and Calvin," 265–281.

[140]Sproul, *Grace Unknown*, 190.

[141]Large Catechism, IV, 28–29, *Triglotta*, 739.

Luther's bold reliance upon the externality of God's aqueous Word of Baptism often shocks Calvinists who spiritualize faith by making it an exclusively internal affair. But as Forde cautions, a faith that has nothing to depend on, or cling to, will feed upon its own internality.[142] Untethered from the sacraments, the saving Word gets sucked into the black hole of the inner self.

It speaks volumes that in two of Sproul's most popular books promoting the heart of Reformed theology, *Grace Unknown* and *What is Reformed Theology?*, the sacraments are not even considered, let alone deserving of their own chapter. They simply do not factor into a Reformed *ordo salutis*, which is why they are not very significant in the life of the Reformed body as a whole.

Sacramental Praxis

The difference in how Lutherans and Calvinists understand the relationship between Word and Sacrament has been one of the leading causes of controversy. Preus observes that in the history of the church, the pendulum has swung back and forth in giving preeminence to one or the other.[143] This is reflected in the architecture and placement of furniture within our respective sanctuaries. In the Roman Mass, the Eucharist is exalted and preaching is but cursory, thus your attention is drawn to the altar alone. In Calvinist churches, the pulpit looms large standing front and center, reflecting the priority of the preached Word. By way of contrast, pulpit and table are held in theological and architectural balance within the Lutheran liturgy as Word and Sacrament buttress one another week in, and week out. As Forde warns, "Without a sacramental understanding of the Word, preaching degenerates into mere information; without preaching, sacraments degenerate into magic."[144]

---

[142]Forde, *Theology is for Proclamation*, 162. His insight on modern self-understanding is very helpful, especially his essay, "Something to Believe," 229–41.

[143]Preus, *A Theology to Live By*, 147.

[144]Forde, *The Preached God*, 100.

The Lord's Supper serves especially as a beneficial extension of the sermon in that it has the advantage of specifying that it is a word specifically "for you." As Luther noted, "This is something more than the congregational sermon; for although the same thing is present in the sermon as in the sacrament, here there is the advantage that it is directed at definite individuals. In the sermon one does not point out or portray any particular person, but in the sacrament it is given to you and to me in particular, so that the sermon comes to be your own."[145]

Lutherans refer to our liturgy as *Gottesdienst* (God's Service), because God is the chief actor moving through his Word and Sacraments to accomplish his gracious purposes. And though I have gone to great lengths to stress the importance of these truths, I must confess that it does not look or sound so exciting to the outside observer sitting in the pew. In fact, it appears to be rather ordinary and uneventful, especially when set in contrast to more popular forms of contemporary evangelical worship. But we should not be surprised by this fact, for it is the humble way of our King. His hometown neighbors once asked about Jesus, "Isn't this Joseph's son?" Luther captures this sentiment well in a sermon where he cautions his listeners against the deception of the eyes:

> There's a big difference between this King and other kings. With the latter everything is outward pomp, great and gallant appearance, magnificent air. But not so with Christ. His mission and work is to help against sin and death, to justify and bring to life. He has placed his help in baptism and the sacrament, and incorporated it in the Word and preaching. To our eyes baptism appears to be nothing more than ordinary water, and the Sacrament of Christ's body and blood simple bread and wine, like other bread and wine, and the sermon, hot air from a man's mouth. But we must not trust what our eyes see, but listen to what this King is teaching us in his Word and Sacrament, namely, I poured out my blood to save you from your sins, to rescue you from death and bring you to heaven; to that end I have given you baptism as a gift for the forgiveness of sins, and preach to you unceasingly by word of mouth concerning this treasure, sealing it to you with the Sacrament of my body and blood, so that you need never

---

[145]Luther, *Sacrament of Christ's Body and Blood*, LW, 36:348.

doubt. True, it seems little and insignificant, that by the washing of water, the Word, and the Sacrament this should all be effected. But don't let your eyes deceive you. At that time, it seemed like a small and insignificant thing for him to come riding on a borrowed donkey and later be crucified, in order to take away sin, death, and hell. No one could tell this by his appearance, but the prophet foretold it, and his work later fulfilled it. Therefore we must simply grasp it with our ears and believe it with our hearts, for our eyes are blind.[146]

Though we may distinguish the various forms of God's external Word, they do not compete for superiority in our liturgy, nor in the life of a believer. All forms of God's Word—oral, scriptural, and sacramental—are cherished and used by our merciful God to confer and strengthen faith. Together they serve the purpose of bringing forgiveness, life, and salvation to sinners in desperate need of God's saving grace.

Lutherans ultimately find their sacramental theology wedged between Calvinism and Catholicism. Scaer comments on this delicate balance:

> Not that Lutheran theology has attempted to find the golden middle, but through its commitment to the Holy Scriptures and its understanding of tradition it has arrived at this position. The Lutheran position is so situated that any movement from its native moorings means slipping into either the Reformed or Roman Catholic attitudes toward the sacraments. If the sacraments are seen as unnecessary so far as the working of God's grace is concerned, the desacramentalized theology of the Reformed has been introduced. If the impression is given that the sacramental actions are really the only necessary constituent factors of the church's existence, then Lutheran theology has adopted a Roman Catholic posture.[147]

In the next three chapters, I shall endeavor to maintain our "native moorings" in the Holy Scriptures as we look at the passages that deal specifically with Baptism and the Lord's Supper.

---

[146]Luther, *House Postils*, 1:28.

[147]Scaer, "Baptism and the Lord's Supper in the Life of the Church," 39.

Baptism Saves

The Washing of Water with the Word

From Noah's floating rescue, to Israel's Red Sea emancipation, to Commander Naaman's Jordan River healing, the Old Testament is saturated with examples of God using water as a vehicle for his saving actions. Therefore, it should come as no surprise that when the prophets spoke of the Messianic age to come, it too would be accompanied by water:

> I will take you from the nations and gather you from all the countries; then I will bring you to your land. 25I will sprinkle you with pure water and you will be clean from all your impurities. I will purify you from all your idols. 26I will give you a new heart, and I will put a new spirit within you. I will remove the heart of stone from your body and give you a heart of flesh. 27I will put my Spirit within you; I will take the initiative and you will obey my statutes and carefully observe my regulations (Ezek 36:24–27).

Nearly four hundred years later, following Jesus' ascension, this Scripture was fulfilled. A large gathering from throughout the Roman Empire had descended upon Jerusalem to celebrate the Feast of Pentecost. There they witnessed the outpouring of the Holy Spirit signifying the dawning of a new age. Peter stood up and preached a moving Christ-centered, redemptive-historical sermon leaving his listeners acutely distressed. "What should we do, brothers?" they asked. Peter answered, "Repent, and each one of you be baptized in the name of Jesus Christ for the forgiveness of your sins, and you will receive the gift of the Holy Spirit" (Acts 2:38). In response, about three thousand were baptized and became members of the infant church. Luke reports the Lord was adding to their number daily those who were being saved (Acts 2:47). Together the Word, Spirit, water, and the forgiveness of sins beautifully coalesced just as God had promised through the prophet Ezekiel.

"No one can read the New Testament," writes Sproul, "even in a cursory manner, and not clearly see that baptism is a very important element of the Christian faith."[148] Lutherans and Calvinists agree that Baptism is the sacrament of initiation commanded by the Lord Jesus as part of the church's disciple-making mission. Both traditions baptize people of all ages, including infants.[149] Furthermore, we both accept that the term *baptizo* is used in the New Testament in a variety of ways—pouring, sprinkling, immersing, dipping, and cleansing— and therefore, neither tradition has stringent rules concerning the particular mode of the water's application in the baptismal rite.[150] Though unified in these areas, Sproul correctly notes that the greatest controversy over baptism has centered on its role in salvation.

Horton argues that the sacraments should be placed in their covenantal context rather than explaining them according to philosophical categories. I agree, but he adds that in their covenantal context, the question is not what the signs themselves do (or don't do), but what the agent executes through these words and signs.[151] While he may not like the question, it is the one I am going to answer in this chapter. *What does baptism do?* Let me be clear. I am not asking what the sign (water) does in and of itself, but what God the agent is executing through baptism, which always includes God's effica-

---

[148]Sproul, *What is Baptism?*, 3.

[149]A full treatment on infant baptism and its relationship to faith in Lutheran thought would warrant an additional chapter, going beyond the scope of this book; however, the reasons here given for the baptism of adults are the same for infants and children.

[150]Though I will disagree significantly with Murray throughout this chapter, he does provide a helpful study on the Bible's use of *baptizo* in his book, *Christian Baptism*, 10–33.

[151]Horton, *Christian Faith*, 778.

cious Word. There is no need for philosophical categories, as we shall examine the biblical passages on their own terms. Since the answer to this question is the primary difference separating Lutherans from Reformed when it comes to baptism, the narrow emphasis of this chapter will be a study of baptismal efficacy drawn from the New Testament passages that explicitly emphasize the soteriological functions of baptism. As we move through the passages that follow, I ask you to keep our two hermeneutical principles at the forefront: interpret Scripture with Scripture and seek the plain meaning of the text. In doing so, I believe the collective weight of the passages, especially when viewed in relation one to another, will prove the Lutheran doctrinal position on baptism to be biblically sound and faithful.

What does Baptism Do?

Baptism Makes Disciples

Matthew 28:18–20

[18]*Then Jesus came up and said to them, "All authority in heaven and on earth has been given to me.* [19]*Therefore go and make disciples of all nations, baptizing them in the name of the Father and the Son and the Holy Spirit,* [20]*teaching them to obey everything I have commanded you. And remember, I am with you always, to the end of the age.*

We begin with the risen Lord's command to make disciples, often referred to as the "great commission," which includes the sacrament of baptism as a necessary component of the disciple-making process. It should be noted that the great commission occurs in each Gospel and at the beginning of Acts prior to Jesus' ascension.[152] The church is sent out to the nations and in the stead and by the command of her Lord she is to proclaim the forgiveness of sins in his name.

---

[152]Mark 16:15–16; Luke 24:46–49; John 20:21; Acts 1:8. The settings and timing of these sayings also vary. A plausible reason for this is that the so-called "great commission" is actually plural, given more than once over the forty day period in a variety of ways to drive the missionary point home.

Three participles are commanded in the commission (v. 19), "Go . . . baptize . . . teach," modifying the imperative verb, "make disciples" (*matheteusate*). Based on this imperative, we must ask, "What is a disciple?" The root of the verb "make disciples" and its cognates is *manthano*, where the essential meaning is to direct one's mind to something. Thus, "disciple" was used in the first century to refer to a follower, a pupil, or one who learns something. The various forms of the word are found most often in the Gospels, where it is applied to the followers of Jesus. Luke uses "disciple" as a synonym for believers (e.g. Acts 14:21). In other words, to be a disciple of Jesus is more than simply learning information about him. Discipleship denotes both adherence and trust, and thus, a positive relationship with Jesus as Master.

How then are disciples made? According to Jesus, disciples are made through baptism and catechesis. The prepositional phrase, "*in* the name of (ESV, NIV, NRSV) . . ." is better translated, "*into* the name of (ASV). . . ." We do not simply baptize on the authority of the Triune God, but rather, "*into* (*eis*) the name (singular) of the Father, Son, and Holy Spirit."[153] Baptism makes a disciple, one who stands in a positive relationship with the Father, Son, and Holy Spirit. The baptized ultimately bear the name of Christ and, therefore, Luke can say, "Now it was in Antioch that the "disciples" were first called "Christians" (Acts 11:26). In other words, a disciple is simply a Christian.

Why did Jesus include baptism in his commission? Sproul answers, "Just as the covenant that God made with Abraham was sealed by the covenant sign of circumcision, so the new covenant that Christ has given to the church is sealed by the sign of baptism."[154] It is common in Reformed theology to refer to the sacraments as "signs" and "seals." While these terms are important and useful, Calvinist theologians strip them of their saving function. For example, Sproul continues, "The sign of God's promise does not guarantee the fulfillment of the promise."[155] Keep in mind that both the promise and command were premised in verse 18 with the declaration that "all

---

[153]So also Hoeksema, *The Triple Knowledge*, 482.

[154]Sproul, *Matthew*, 826.

[155]Sproul, *Truths We Confess*, 3:115.

authority in heaven and earth" had been given to Jesus. Is this not the Messiah, the very Son of God, making the promise and commanding the means by which disciples are made? The sign of God's promise does not guarantee the fulfillment of the promise? Is Jesus incapable of making good on his promise? Sproul is repeating a long history of Calvinist scholarship on the nature of signs and seals.

John Murray provides another example:

> Equally pertinent is the observation that which is signified or sealed does not bring into existence that which is signified or sealed. It does not effect union with Christ. In other words, baptism does not convey or confer the grace which it signifies.[156]

What then is baptism good for if it does not actually make one a disciple as Jesus clearly promises? Murray answers, "He [God] not only unites His people to Christ but also advertises that great truth by an ordinance which portrays visibly to our senses the reality of this grace."[157] According to Murray, baptism acts as an advertisement of grace, but it does not supply it. Like a street sign, it points elsewhere. The difficulty for the Calvinist position is that we get no sense here, or elsewhere, of baptism functioning as a billboard on the religious interstate advertising a gracious God. The difference between our two traditions on the nature of sacramental signs can be summarized by a common illustration that Sproul often uses.[158] I am writing this chapter in San Diego, California. If you were to travel south on Interstate 5 from Los Angeles you would pass numerous signs pointing out the distance to San Diego. For example, when you reach the city of Carlsbad, the sign reads, "San Diego–42 miles." This is the type of sign that Calvinists have in mind concerning the sacraments. As Sproul says, "It points beyond itself to something else. In the same way, baptism is not salvation and all that it entails."[159] But

---

[156]Murray, *Christian Baptism*, 86. See also, Westminster Confession, 28.1.

[157]Murray, *Christian Baptism*, 87.

[158]Sproul, *What is Baptism?*, 31–32. I have personalized the geography, but the illustration remains the same.

[159]Sproul, *What is Baptism?*, 32.

if you were to continue driving to the city limits of San Diego, you will see another sign, "Welcome to San Diego." This is the Lutheran understanding of baptism as sacramental sign and symbol. It is a visible sign, but it points to a reality that is actually present. As a symbol, it actually participates in that which it symbolizes. The marquee "Welcome to San Diego" participates and constitutes San Diego as such. We need not look elsewhere for Christ's promise or presence for it encompasses the reality of it.

Likewise, Calvinists speak of baptism as a "seal." Sproul follows Calvin's logic by using the analogy of a king or government official stamping his seal of approval upon an important document.

> In the ancient world, the seal was the symbol of ownership, of authenticity, and of authority. When a king sent out an edict or an official communication of some kind, the document was sealed with a drop of hot wax, and the king pressed his signet ring into the wax, giving it his mark or brand to prove its authenticity. In the same way, the gift of the Spirit seals the believer, for God gives His Spirit only to those who are His.[160]

The analogy works if the sealed edict actually has something written on it. But once more, in a Reformed sacramental view, "baptism is not salvation and all that it entails." What grace is the seal actually confirming in baptism if it does not entail the grace of salvation? Baptism has become a divine scavenger hunt in Calvinism, with Jesus authoritatively sealing a letter, but when opened, it reads the following:

Dear Baptismal Candidate,

Please go back to the pew and await further direction in the sermon, for the Holy Spirit and the forgiveness of sins is not to be found here at this font as you may have surmised from the testimony of my apostles and inspired writers regarding Baptism.

Yours truly,
King Jesus

---

[160]Sproul, *What is Baptism?*, 48. See also, Calvin, *Institutes*, 4.14.5.

Is it not more faithful to accept the plain reading of Matthew's Gospel? The frontier sacrament of baptism places one into the family of the Holy Trinity, thus making all who are baptized disciples of Christ. Scaer summarizes this Trinitarian movement:

> The Creator who became incarnate in Jesus becomes one with the sacramental elements. The Spirit who moved over the face of the waters wraps himself in the water to make it a baptism. Jesus' going to God's right hand was not a spatial movement. Rather he entered the church's sacramental life with his Spirit to exercise divine power in reconciling sinners to God. For Luther, in Baptism "God's grace, the entire Christ, and the Holy Spirit with His gifts" are present (LC IV, 41).[161]

There is a personal encounter with the Holy Trinity as he unites us to himself through his watery word. And just as a newborn needs milk (and eventually solid food as she matures), so too does the baptized child of God need instruction. Thus, Jesus includes catechesis as part of the disciple-making commission. This is significant considering that access to education under a notable rabbi was normally reserved for men of privileged status. Wilkins states the radical nature of Christian discipleship in a first century context:

> Some rabbis denied young girls even the basics of Torah instruction, such as Eliezar who said: "If any man gives his daughter knowledge of the Law it is as though he taught her lechery" (*m. Sotah* 3:4). But Jesus once again breaks down barriers to indicate that all of his disciples—women and men, Gentile and Jew, poor and rich—are to be taught to obey everything he has commanded. But the emphasis is not simply on acquisition of knowledge. The goal of instructing new disciples of Jesus is obedience to what he has commanded, so that their lives increasingly become like their Master.[162]

The church can take comfort in her disciple-making mission, because we are not left alone, as if our success was dependent upon

---

[161]Scaer, "Holy Spirit, Sacraments, and Church Rites," 318.

[162]Wilkins, "Matthew," *ZIBBC*, 190.

our gifts and abilities. The last reassuring words from the King offer another promise, "And remember, I am with you always, even to the end of the age" (Matt 28:20). The personal pronoun "I" here designates the whole person—both Christ's divine and human natures. Through baptism (and the Lord's Supper) the ascended King maintains his presence with his people.

Baptism Saves

Mark 16:15–16

[15]*He said to them, "Go into all the world and preach the gospel to every creature.* [16]*The one who believes and is baptized will be saved, but the one who does not believe will be condemned.*

Here in the "great commission" of Mark's contested longer ending we are given two participles that describe who will be saved. The aorist participles—the one who "believes" and is "baptized"—represent past actions in relation to the time of the verb, "shall be saved" (*sothesetai*). They are united under one article, connecting the reception of the gospel to faith and baptism. The passive voice of the future verb translated, "shall be saved," confirms that God is the one doing the saving. Wessel comments, "As the Gospel is for all, so baptism is for all. Being baptized is here taught as a proof of a person's faith in the gospel of the crucified and risen Christ."[163] For example, the Ethiopian Eunuch said to Phillip, "Look, there is water! What is to stop me from being baptized?" (Acts 8:36). The Ethiopian's response proves that Phillip must have stressed the necessity of baptism while he taught him about Christ's identity from the prophet Isaiah.

Mark also includes the negative response to the church's Gospel mission. "He who does not believe will be condemned." It is not the lack of baptism that condemns, but the lack of faith. There is, therefore, no need for Jesus to mention baptism, since the one rejecting Christ will naturally reject his sacrament. But the promise remains, "the one who believes and is baptized will be saved." Luther concludes:

---

[163]Wessel, *Proof Texts of the Catechism*, 2:79.

This is the most simple way to put it: The power, effects, benefit, fruit, and purpose of baptism is that it saves. For no one is baptized in order to become a prince, but, as the words say, "to be saved." To be saved, as everyone well knows, is nothing else than to be delivered from sin, death, and the devil, to enter into Christ's kingdom, and to live with him forever.[164]

Reformed and Baptist pastors have on occasion confronted me with the particular word order found here in Mark. Since belief is placed prior to baptism, they reason they have the doctrinal upper hand, but I remind them that Matthew reverses the order, placing baptism first. For Lutherans, the particular sequence of faith and baptism is not necessary for a valid baptism. Luther said that it makes no difference whether faith precedes or follows baptism, so long as faith is present.[165]

1 Peter 3:21

[21]*And this prefigured baptism, which now saves you—not the washing off of physical dirt but the pledge of a good conscience to God—through the resurrection of Jesus Christ . . .*

Peter provides what at face value is a straightforward statement on the purpose of baptism by linking it to Noah's rescue. Baptism saves! This letter is written to bring encouragement to believers who are suffering for their faith. He draws upon the experience of Jesus' suffering (3:13–17) in order to embolden his readers to persevere in the midst of suffering for Christ's sake (3:18–22). Peter can offer this hope solely on the basis of Christ's victorious resurrection and ascension where he now reigns as the triumphant King at the right hand of the Father (3:21–22). All Christians share in this resurrection victory. How? Through "baptism, which now saves you" (3:21).

There is a typological correspondence between the flood story of Genesis and the New Testament sacrament of baptism. Because of the length and complexity of the Greek sentence, translators break

---

[164]Large Catechism, IV, 24–25, *Book of Concord* (Kolb-Wengert), 459.

[165]Luther, *Concerning Rebaptism*, LW, 40:252–54.

this verse into separate sentences in English. Verse 21 literally reads, "which also, [as] an antitype, now saves you, [that is] baptism." Just as Noah and his family were delivered through water from God's wrath upon an evil world, so Christians have been saved from the judgment to come through the saving waters of baptism.

Because Peter's unambiguous description of baptism as a saving act is troubling for Reformed exegetes, Sproul attempts to muddy the waters by diverting our attention to the fact that Noah was saved by the ark, and not through water:

> The salvation that is described as taking place through water indicates that water was the instrument of salvation for Noah and his family. If you look at that story of Noah, you see that the water for those who perished was the cause of their destruction. It was the instrument of divine wrath against a world that had gone over completely into godlessness. At the same time, those very waters that destroyed the world carried the vessel in which the family of Noah was housed and carried them to safety. Notice that, with reference to baptism, Peter does not say that the eight were immersed in water. The ones who were immersed perished. The ones who were carried above the water were saved.[166]

This is certainly true, of course, but it does nothing to change the fact that under the inspiration of the Holy Spirit, Peter says they were "delivered through water" (v. 20). It is the antecedent of the flood waters that furnishes the basis for the properties which Peter now attributes to baptism. The word "antitype" in verse 21 is used to express a copy of an original.[167] The type or original in this case is baptism. Here we find a continuity of God's saving actions in both the Old and New Testament, but also discontinuity, in that baptism is specifically joined to Christ's resurrection. How does baptism save? It is not by the "removal of physical dirt from the flesh, but through the pledge of a

---

[166]Sproul, *1–2 Peter*, 133.

[167]This word is extremely rare as its only other use in the New Testament is Heb 9:24. Varying English translations—*prefigures* (NET), *corresponds* (ESV), and especially, *symbolizes* (NIV)—all fail to capture the full meaning of "antitype."

good conscience to God—through the resurrection of Jesus Christ." In other words, baptism is not simply an outward, fleshly removal akin to circumcision, but a sacramental cleansing that positively affects the believer's conscience. The word "conscience" (*suneideseos*) should not be understood as a subjective feeling of guilt or innocence, as is common today, but rather, as an expression of awareness. To summarize, baptism saves, because through this cleansing water we are able to approach God with a good conscience. It is not our pledge to God, but God's pledge of a good conscience to us (cf. Heb 10:22).

In his commentary, Sproul enlists Aristotle's theory of causality in an attempt to undermine any interpretation that suggests the sacrament of baptism was instituted to be an "instrumental cause" of salvation. In order to protect the doctrine of justification by faith alone against Roman sacerdotalism, it is remarkable that the services of this particular Greek philosopher are employed to explain away the plain reading of the passage.[168]

Using the example of an artist, Sproul says the instrumental cause is what the artist uses to bring about a finished work. For a painter, it is his brushes. The "efficient cause" is the painter himself, since the instruments cannot function on their own. Sproul concludes that for Protestants the instrumental cause of justification is faith, which then excludes baptism from being an instrument of grace.[169] However, this seems to run contrary to Sproul's own confessional standard. The Westminster divines argued that God's eternal decree does not cancel the "liberty or contingency of secondary causes, but actually establishes them."[170] In other words, God is free to use his creation to accomplish his will, thus making them instrumental causes in that they actually do what he desires. In the flood story, Noah and his family were delivered, while the rest drowned. God remains the efficient cause behind the flood waters as the creative artist, while the

---

[168]See Sproul, *1–2 Peter*, 133–134. This is not only completely unnecessary, but strikes me as being apologetically selective, seeing that the Roman Catholic doctrine of transubstantiation is largely dependent upon Aristotle's metaphysical categories, which Sproul refutes elsewhere, *What is Reformed Theology*, 85–86.

[169]Sproul, *Truths We Confess*, 3:95.

[170]Westminster Confession, III, 1.

instrument he chose to accomplish his dual work of judgment (Law) and salvation (Gospel) was water. So it is with Baptism. The Holy Spirit is the efficient cause of cleansing the sinner, and one way he does so is through the sacramental instrument of baptism, gifting the faith that justifies (new birth). What Sproul fails to grasp is that baptism and faith are not in competition with one another. One begets the other. They are both gifts of God and the instruments of his creative will. After all, a painter rarely uses just one brush.

In verse 20, the passive form of "deliverance" reminds us again that God is the subject doing the rescuing verbs through his appointed means. Baptism is not our work, but God's divine speech-act comprehended in water. Luther said, "For to be baptized in the name of God is to be baptized not by man but by God himself. Therefore, although it is performed by human hands, it is nevertheless truly God's own work."[171] Like Noah and his family, we are passive recipients as God delivers us through the water by the power of his promissory word. Faith lays hold of Christ through baptism, thus preserving justification by faith alone (*sola fide*).

Sproul concludes that it is a mistake to assume that baptism indicates salvation.[172] But I ask, "What does Peter actually say?" Presbyterian theologian, Peter Leithart, wryly admits, "It is not as if Peter says, 'baptism now saves you,' and then adds, as a slight nuance, 'but baptism doesn't really save you.'"[173] Luther addresses Sproul's concern in his Small Catechism concerning the water of Baptism:

How can water do such great things?

Answer: It is not the water indeed that does them, but the word of God which is in and with the water, and faith, which trusts such word of God in the water. For without the word of God the water is simple water and no baptism. But with the word of God it is a baptism, that is, a gracious water of life and a washing of regeneration in the Holy Ghost.[174]

---

[171]Large Catechism, IV, 10, *Triglotta*, 735.

[172]Sproul, *1–2 Peter*, 137.

[173]Leithart, *Baptized Body*, 30.

[174]Small Catechism, IV, 3, *Triglotta*, 551.

As Peter consoles his troubled readers by reminding them of baptism's saving efficacy, it robs faith of nothing; rather, it gives their faith something tangible to lay hold of in the midst of persecution. Despite their present suffering, they remain the baptized. Though their earthly goods may be plundered or worse, no one can take back what God has done for them in their baptism. Far from just picturing deliverance, God has actually delivered.

Baptism Works Forgiveness of Sins

Acts 2:37–39

37Now when they heard this, they were acutely distressed and said to Peter and the rest of the apostles, "What should we do, brothers? 38Peter said to them, "Repent, and each of you be baptized in the name of Jesus Christ for the forgiveness of your sins, and you will receive the gift of the Holy Spirit. For the promise is for you and your children, and for all who are far away, as many as the Lord our God will call to himself."

In the book of Acts, Luke provides several conversion narratives where he clearly demonstrates how the early church stressed the functional significance and importance of baptism. Two examples will suffice in demonstrating how he connects baptism to the forgiveness of sins.[175]

Jesus promised the disciples when he went away he would send the Spirit who would guide them into all truth (John 16:13). As noted in the introduction, this promise was fulfilled on the day of Pentecost when the disciples were filled with the Holy Spirit. When the guilt-ridden crowd sought a remedy for their sin, Peter commanded them to repent and be baptized for the forgiveness of sins, where they would receive the gift of the Holy Spirit.

Calvinism denies that the two-fold gift of forgiveness and the endowment of the Holy Spirit can be tethered to baptism. In his commentary, Calvin says we must "beware that we tie not the grace of God to the sacraments; for the external administration of baptism

---

[175]For more, see Acts 8:5–13, 8:35–39, 9:1–18, 10:34–48, 16:13–15, 16:30–34, 18:8, and 19:1–7.

profiteth nothing."[176] Sproul is just as adamant, "The sacraments have never saved anyone, and anyone who puts his trust in the sacraments has a false assurance of salvation, because he is trusting in something that neither saves nor can save."[177] This passage, quite obviously, presents some exegetical difficulties for such a position. Some Reformed and Baptist scholars have proposed that the preposition *eis*, in the phrase, "for the forgiveness of sins," should be translated, "on account of," or, "because" our sins have already been remitted. Thus, they can maintain that baptism merely pictures outwardly what is already true of those who repent inwardly.[178] There are several problems with this suggestion.

First, the preposition *eis* never means "because" in Greek. Rather, it is used to indicate the movement toward a goal or to denote purpose.[179] Lenski argues that it is either the grammatical difference of sphere, or aim and purpose.

> Sphere would mean that baptism is inside the same circle as remission; he who steps into this circle has both. Aim and purpose would mean that baptism intends to give remission; in him, then, who receives baptism aright this intention, aim, and purpose would be attained. The same is true regarding the idea of effect in *eis*. This preposition connects remission so closely with baptism that nobody has as yet been able to separate the two. It is this gift or remission that makes baptism a true sacrament; otherwise it would be only a sign or a symbol that conveys nothing real.[180]

Second, there is a sacramental parallel in the Lord's Supper with the same prepositional phrase, ". . . this is my blood of the covenant which is poured out for many *for the forgiveness of sins*" (Matt 26:28). Did Jesus shed his blood "for" the forgiveness of our sins, or "because" of the forgiveness we already possess? Clearly, it is the former and all

---

[176]Calvin, *Commentaries*, 19:303.

[177]Sproul, *Can I Be Sure I'm Saved?*, 40.

[178]Thomas, *Acts*, 49.

[179]See Bauer, *Greek-English Lexicon of the New Testament*, 228–232.

[180]Lenski, *Acts*, 107–108.

Reformed exegetes accept that *eis* means "for" in this passage; thus I find the retranslation of Peter's use in Acts questionable.

Baptism, forgiveness, and the Holy Spirit function paradigmatically in Luke–Acts. Peter's command for repentance and baptism in Christ's name is analogous to John the Baptist's preaching of repentance and baptism that directed his listeners to Christ as the Lamb of God. To the gathered crowd at the Jordan River, John states, "I baptize you with water, but one more powerful than I am is coming—I am not worthy to untie the strap of his sandals. He will baptize you with the Holy Spirit and fire" (Luke 3:16). We find this Trinitarian relationship most clearly in Jesus' own baptism where the Holy Spirit descends, anointing the King for his mission, and the Father's voice confirming the sonship of the Lord, as Jesus assumed responsibility for the sin of the world (Luke 3:21–23).

Peter announces the fulfillment of Joel's prophecy of the Spirit being poured out and deliverance for all who call upon the name of the Lord (Joel 2:28–32). Baptism not only brings forgiveness in Jesus' name, but the accompanying gift of the Holy Spirit as the two are inseparable. And this promise is not only for adult converts, but for our children as well, "For the promise is for you and your children, and for all who are far away, as many as the Lord our God will call to himself" (v. 39).

Acts 22:16

[16]*And now what are you waiting for? Get up, be baptized, and have your sins washed away, calling on his name.*

In one concise statement, Paul recounts the command of Ananias to be baptized, where he was promised his sins would be washed away. To "baptize" and to "wash away" are similar in meaning. Cleansing is what the material element of water naturally does. Ananias did not command two things, but one: be baptized. The "washing away" of sins is explanatory. It is the result of being baptized.

The imagery of baptism as a washing of sin is a truth Paul will later employ in his own letters. For example, he demarcates the Corinthian's pre-Christian lives by virtue of their baptism. "Some of you once lived this way. But you were *washed*, you were sanctified, you were justified in the name of the Lord Jesus Christ and by the Spirit of our God" (1 Cor 6:11, italics mine). Note how Paul connects baptism to sanctification, justification, Christ's name, and the Holy Spirit. Together it echoes the baptismal formulas found throughout Acts. This is not to suggest a definitive *ordo*, but to affirm the numerous gospel blessings encompassed in the washing of baptism. Later in the same epistle he links baptism to the Spirit and the unity of the church, "For in one Spirit we were all baptized into one body. Whether Jews or slaves or free, we were all made to drink of the one Spirit" (1 Cor 12:13).

The Old Testament story of the Syrian army commander, Naaman, provides another clear example of how God has used the washing of water and the power of his Word to bring cleansing (2 Kings 5:1–14). Naaman was afflicted with leprosy and was directed by his wife's maidservant to seek healing from the prophet Elisha in Israel. When Naaman arrived at the prophet's house, he was told to wash in the Jordan seven times, with the promise that he would be restored and cleansed. Naaman, in Calvinist fashion, was put off by the very thought of God using the means of water as an instrument of healing. He complained, "Look, I thought for sure he would come out, stand there, invoke the name of the Lord his God, wave his hand over the area, and cure the skin disease" (v. 11). Naaman eventually submitted to the prophet's command, "Wash and you will be clean" (v. 13).

There are several connections to Paul's baptism in Acts. The Septuagint's version of Naaman's story translates the Hebrew words identically to the Greek of Ananias' baptismal command in Acts 22:16.[181] But more important than lexical similarities is that we have another irrefutable instance where water has the power to cleanse, not because of Namaan's faith, but because of the Word of the Lord given through the prophet. Bender summarizes this nicely:

> This story teaches us that the power of the baptismal water lies in the Word and promise of Christ the Lord. He is the saving content of

---

[181]The Septuagint is an early Greek translation of the Old Testament. As an example, when Naaman "dipped" himself in the Jordan, the Hebrew *tabal* is translated with the Greek *baptizo*.

the water of baptism, and by His Word the Spirit of God communicates those benefits to us in Baptism. This story also teaches us that it is the word of God alone which breaks the hardness of the sinful heart, so that it believes in the promise of Baptism and receives the salvation and cleansing which Baptism contains.[182]

Calvin assumes that Paul is already converted with saving faith; otherwise, Ananias would never have commanded baptism. He presumptuously asserts that Luke, for efficiencies sake, passed over a good deal of pertinent instruction in this summary, and cautions against putting any confidence in the outward sign of baptism.[183] In a more recent Reformed apology for baptism amidst competing views, Presbyterian scholar, Pratt admits, "As central as baptism is to the doctrine of salvation, we must never allow anyone to rest his or her hopes for eternal salvation on the rite of baptism."[184] Can you imagine Paul responding to Ananias with such unbelief? What the Reformed offer with one hand (*it's central*), they take away with the other (*no, not really, we cannot rest our hopes on it*). Once more, the symbolic interpretation is left wanting when set against the clear teaching of Holy Scripture. The washing away of sin, according to Ananias' command, is the result of being baptized. Lutherans do not rest our hopes in the water, but in the One who commanded the water be used to apply the benefits of his death and resurrection.

Baptism Unites us to Christ

Romans 6:3–5

³Or do you not know that as many as were baptized into Christ Jesus were baptized into his death? ⁴Therefore we have been buried with him through baptism into death, in order that just as Christ was raised from the dead through the glory of the Father, so we too may live a new

---

[182]Bender, *Lutheran Catechesis*, 218.

[183]Calvin, *Commentaries*, 19:302. So also, Godfrey, "Why Baptism?," 27–28.

[184]Pratt, "Reformed View," *Four Views*, 121.

life. ⁵For if we have been united with him in the likeness of his death, we will certainly also be united in the likeness of his resurrection.

For Paul the sacrament of baptism is always bound up in, with, and through the death and resurrection of Christ. Therefore, Paul can appeal in 6:3 to baptism as a fixed event that brought death to the old Adam, an end to the reign of sin, and renewal to the lives of his readers. Those who have been baptized into Christ Jesus have been baptized into his death, and therefore, have broken with the past. Baptism teaches a crucial truth about justification. According to Paulson:

> It is not exoneration, improvement, alteration, or cleaning off the old Adam . . . A new heart is not a change of heart, but a new creation *ex nihilo*. Baptism is therefore death and new life, which reverses the sort of living anticipated in the legal scheme [Torah]. Without baptism we live with death looming in front of us; with baptism we live ecstatically, death lies behind us and life blooms like an opening flower ahead.[185]

If death signifies a break with our former life in Adam, resurrection ushers us into the life of Christ. We find a parallel in Colossians, "Having been buried with him in baptism, you also have been raised with him through your faith in the power of God who raised him from the dead" (Col 2:12). According to Paul, baptism unites us to Christ. The majority of Reformed commentators, especially Calvin, have much to say about this union. But the most they are willing to allow baptism is that it "signifies" or "symbolizes" the union, but does not in any way effect it.[186] The language Paul employs, however, is instrumental in character, which means it actually seals the union by incorporating us into Christ. As a means of grace, baptism functions as a vehicle to move us from one location to another. In the case of baptism, the Pauline prepositions show our locatedness (i.e. in, into, and with Christ). The baptized are no longer Adam-people but, by a divine transference, Christ-people, members of his kingdom,

---

[185]Paulson, *Lutheran Theology*, 157.

[186]For example, Hagopian, *Back to Basics*, 180.

whose terms of existence are defined, not by Adam's disobedience, but by Christ's perfect obedience and his imputed righteousness.[187]

Commenting upon baptism as a sign of death and resurrection, Sproul writes, "As you can see, baptism is full of rich symbolism that points to all the things God does for us when He delivers us from our sin."[188] But Paul is not painting a symbolic word-picture. He is stating a past tense fact, "we have been buried with him *through* baptism into death," in order to contrast our present tense reality, "so we too may *walk* in newness of life."[189] Paul appeals to his readers' baptismal union with Christ as the reason that sin should no longer reign (v. 13). It is because of this that Luther stressed the life-long significance of baptism. He does not say, "I *was* baptized," but rather, "I *am* baptized." In the Large Catechism, Luther writes, "Therefore every Christian has enough in Baptism to learn and to practice all his life; for he has always enough to do to believe firmly what it promises and brings: victory over death and the devil, forgiveness of sin, the grace of God, the entire Christ, and the Holy Ghost with his gifts."[190]

Senkbeil captures the heart of this passage, "We're all dying; we can either die alone, or we can die in Jesus. But his death brings life, and it's when we die with him that we really begin to live."[191] Far from functioning as an empty symbol, Paul asserts that baptism effects a sacramental union of the baptized with the death, burial, and resurrection of Christ.

Galatians 3:26–28

[26]*For in Christ Jesus you are all sons of God through faith.* [27]*For all of you who were baptized into Christ have clothed yourselves with Christ.* [28]*There is neither Jew nor Greek, there is neither slave nor free, there is neither male nor female—for all of you are one in Christ Jesus.*

---

[187]Westerholm, *Understanding Paul*, 108.

[188]Sproul, *What is Baptism?*, 47.

[189]The verb "walk" (*peripatesomen*) is aorist subjunctive in form, indicating the entirety of the Christian pilgrimage from baptism until biological death (or Christ's return).

[190]Large Catechism, IV, 41, *Triglotta*, 743.

[191]Senkbeil, *Dying to Live*, 55.

What greater privilege can a sinner receive than to be identified as a son of God? "Like any good parent," Kolb observes, "God is concerned about clothing his children."[192] Paul is emphatic throughout Galatians that we belong to the household of God, not by works of the law, but through faith. The apostle can say this of the Galatian Christians, even in the midst of their struggle to understand the gospel aright, because they have been baptized.

Here Paul settles the question, "Who are the rightful heirs of the Abrahamic promise?" He answers it is those who have been baptized and clothed with Christ. The action of being clothed constitutes a major motif in the Bible, going back to the very beginning. Adam and Eve's eyes were opened to recognize their nakedness when they committed high treason in the garden. They tried covering themselves with fig leaves in a futile effort of works righteousness, but God in his mercy, "clothed" them with garments from skin (Gen 3:21). Isaiah thus spoke of salvation as being clothed by God, "I will greatly rejoice in the Lord; my soul shall exult in my God, for he has clothed me with the garments of salvation; he has covered me with the robe of righteousness, as a bridegroom decks himself like a priest with a beautiful headdress, and as a bride adorns herself with her jewels" (Is 61:10).

Paul is employing this same scriptural motif to show how God clothes us with Christ in baptism—imputing to us his life, righteousness, and name. Just as God covered the shame of Adam and Eve in the garden, he has covered us with his own Son. "To impute," according to Zahl, "means to ascribe qualities to someone that are not there intrinsically, to regard somebody as a person that he or she is not."[193] By means of baptism, in other words, God calls the spiritual orphan a son or daughter. Nonbelievers traverse through life like Jason Bourne, asking, "Who am I?" But Paul says the baptized can know for certain they are an adopted child of God, an heir who now has the Spirit of the Son in their hearts and can call on God in the most intimate manner, "Abba! Father!" (Gal 4:6). Preus notes the significance of Paul's adoption metaphor:

---

[192]Kolb, *Christian Faith*, 220.

[193]Zahl, *Grace in Practice*, 119.

Through Baptism, God has gathered His disparate creatures and brought them into His household. He has adopted us, declared us to be His children. Now we know who we are because we know whose we are. Now we are cherished, wanted, desired, acknowledged by our Father. Now we have full rights of children. No longer are we slaves of an evil taskmaster, objects of wrath. Now we know that God loves us. Because we know this, we may now live as children of God, as those born of God.[194]

Reformed theologian, Ridderbos, cautions that we should not take Paul's reference to baptism in a magical or automatic sense. He argues, "What happens at baptism is a confirmation and sealing, a visible manifestation of what is given to the church by faith."[195] Once more we find a Calvinist anxious about separating faith from baptism, lest we grant baptism too much saving power. But in this very passage, Paul speaks comfortably of both, not in opposition to one another, but in a cooperative and instrumental sense of one begetting the other. To assuage those who, like Ridderbos, fear Lutherans may ascribe to baptism magical characteristics, I must repeat that Luther did not treat the gift of baptism or speak of grace in the form of a magical spell or infused substance. On the contrary:

Grace means the favor by which God accepts us, forgiving sins and justifying freely through Christ. It belongs to the category of relationship . . . So you should not think it is a quality, as the scholastics dreamed . . . But the true Spirit dwells in believers not merely according to his gifts, but according to his own substance. He does not give his gifts in such a way that he is somewhere else or asleep, but he is present with his gifts.[196]

Thus, Scaer can say, "The baptismal state of pure grace is perfectly complimented by a faith which puts its total trust in the One

---

[194]Preus, *Just Words*, 126.

[195]Ridderbos, *Galatians*, 148.

[196]Luther, *Select Psalms*, LW, 12:377. Emphasis mine.

present in baptism."[197] Grace, as Luther notes, falls into the category of a relationship. We find as Paul continues, our relational identity as the baptized in Christ is more radical and fundamental than race, class, or gender. *For there is neither Jew nor Greek, there is neither slave nor free, there is neither male nor female—for all of you are one in Christ Jesus.* Vanhoozer notes the significance, "Being a Christian is not incidental to our being, then, like being Californian, white, or left-handed. On the contrary, far from being a mere accident or add-on to something already substantial, our union with Christ defines our very being."[198] Those who have been clothed with Christ, despite their background, have entered Abraham's family tree. The baptized are heirs according to promise (v. 29).

Baptism Regenerates

John 3:5

[5]*Jesus answered, "I tell you the solemn truth, unless a person is born of water and spirit, he cannot enter the kingdom of God."*

When Nicodemus sought out Jesus under the cover of night, he is told that no one can enter the kingdom of God unless he is born again of water and Spirit. Although a highly developed baptismal theology is woven everywhere into the fabric of John's Gospel, according to Scaer it requires what may appear to the modern reader to be a high degree of sophistication to decipher the vocabulary.[199] This certainly was not the case in the early church, but because John is not as explicit as the synoptics with a command to baptize, less sacramentally inclined commentators debate whether John's use of Spirit, water, and birth can be understood as baptismal terms. For example, Calvin acknowledges that the greater part of the Christian tradition, including Chrysostom, had understood this passage to be about baptism, but concludes that such an interpretation is inappropriate as the term water is nothing more than the inward purification

---

[197]Scaer, "Baptism and the Lord's Supper," 44.

[198]Vanhoozer, *Drama of Doctrine*, 394.

[199]Scaer, *Discourses in Matthew*, 151.

and invigoration which is produced by the Holy Spirit, and should be understood as a synonym for the Spirit.[200] Because Calvin radically breaks with the historic position of the church by disconnecting the new birth of the Holy Spirit from baptism, he forces an unnatural reading upon the text. Beasley-Murray refutes Calvin's interpretation exegetically by noting that "from above" in verses 3 and 7 apply to "water and the Spirit" and not to the Spirit alone. He concludes that Calvin's preference for understanding water as the Spirit came from his utter distaste for baptismal conversion.[201]

Presbyterian pastor, Boice, goes further afield as he rejects that Jesus is even referring to baptism at all. He argues that "water" should be understood as a metaphor for the Bible by citing Ephesians 5:26 (*washing of water by the word*) as a supposed parallel to support his very novel interpretation.[202] But as I will later demonstrate, Paul is clearly speaking of the sanctifying benefits of baptism that are never without God's Word.

There was no question in Luther's mind that "water and Spirit" referred to the church's Sacrament of Holy Baptism, as the theme of water interlaces the first three chapters of the Fourth Gospel.[203] Water is mentioned in chapter one to contrast John's baptism with Jesus' baptism of the Holy Spirit (1:19–34). Next Jesus turns the six stone jars of water normally reserved for the Jewish rite of purification into wine (2:1–11), thus transforming the way purification was to be understood. These two examples reach a confluence in chapter three. Koester explains John's unique literary structure:

> We have already seen how the evangelist initially made the suggestive observation that Nicodemus came to Jesus "by night" (3:2), but

---

[200]Calvin, *Commentaries*, 17:110. Leon Morris's widely influential commentary in evangelical circles echoes Calvin's reading. At least Calvin is willing to concede that by neglecting baptism, we are excluded from salvation (and in this sense, he acknowledges its necessity).

[201]Beasley-Murray, *Baptism in the New Testament*, 228, n. 2.

[202]Boice, *John*, 1:245.

[203]For more on the Johannine water motif, see Koester, *Symbolism in the Fourth Gospel*, 176–206.

did not disclose the significance of the darkness until later (3:19–21). Similarly, water is mentioned only briefly in connection with new birth (3:5), but its import is made clearer in the subsequent discussion of baptism (3:22–26). The conclusion of the chapter reiterates the themes mentioned earlier—belief and unbelief, above and below, testimony, the Spirit, and eternal life—helping to integrate the parts of this chapter into a whole (3:31–36).[204]

It makes complete sense that the two previously mentioned aspects of water would come together in discussion with Nicodemus, a Pharisee and leader in Jerusalem, the group that sent a delegation to question John about his baptismal practices (1:19, 24; 3:1). As Scaer observes the pericope of Nicodemus is informative in that Jesus, the one ushering in God's kingdom is personally present; nevertheless the Jewish leader must be born of water and the Spirit to share in the kingdom's benefits. Even with Jesus present there can be no detour around baptism's water.[205]

According to Jesus, the new birth comes not merely by water, or merely by the Spirit, but by water *and* Spirit. I must reiterate the power in baptism is not found in the water itself, but in God the Holy Spirit bringing new birth from above, comprehended in the sacramental rite (which by its very command must include water and Word). John's grammar further supports this reading. First, "of" (*ek*) denotes origin and source. The fact that there is one preposition makes water and Spirit a single concept. Second, the absence of the Greek article with the two nouns makes their unity even more apparent. The single concept containing both water and Spirit can be nothing other than baptism in the New Testament.

A theological caveat is here required since the very mention of baptismal regeneration is anathema to Calvinists. For example, Murray calls it is a sacerdotalist conception that is not worth his effort to refute in any extended manner.[206] For Lutherans baptismal

---

[204]Koester, *Symbolism in the Fourth Gospel*, 183.

[205]Scaer, "Baptism and the Lord's Supper," 41.

[206]Murray, *Christian Baptism*, 86, f.n. 44. It is noteworthy that this passage and the next (Titus 3:5) are completely omitted from his chapter on the efficacy of baptism, which speaks volumes.

regeneration is not identical with the Roman Catholic notion of the *opus operatum*, which is to say, baptismal regeneration does not occur automatically or magically apart from faith. On the contrary, as I have argued, it is the work of the Holy Spirit to impart saving faith, and he does so, in baptism, as a sacramental work of God. Just as you had no control over your physical birth, so it is with your spiritual rebirth. Luther corrected the medieval doctrine of baptism by bringing it in line with his doctrine of justification.[207] Time and again Luther emphasized that baptism carries a divine promise of salvation, and where there is a divine promise, there faith is required. Hence, to seek the efficacy of the sacrament apart from the promise and faith is to labor in vain and to find condemnation.[208] This does not mean, however, that the validity of baptism depends on a person's faith. Baptism is God's work and, as such, does not exclude faith. "Faith does not make baptism," Luther said, "but receives it."[209] Reformed historian, Godfrey, acknowledges the same. "Faith does not create the promise of God. God's promise comes before faith and through faith. Nevertheless, faith receives the sacrament unto blessings."[210]

I often ask my Reformed friends who are troubled by the idea of baptismal regeneration, "If the Holy Spirit is in no way tethered to baptism, does this then mean that the Holy Spirit brings new birth immediately apart from all external means?" Their answer, of course, is no. The Heidelberg Catechism confirms:

> Q 65: Since then we are made partakers of Christ and all his benefits by faith only, whence does this faith proceed?
>
> Answer: From the Holy Ghost, who works faith in our hearts by the preaching of the Gospel, and confirms it by the use of the sacraments.

---

[207] Paul Althaus was correct when he wrote that Luther's doctrine of baptism is basically nothing else than his doctrine of justification in concrete form, *Theology of Martin Luther*, 356.

[208] Luther, *Babylonian Captivity*, LW, 36:67.

[209] Large Catechism, IV, 53, *Book of Concord* (Kolb-Wengert), 463.

[210] Godfrey, "Why Baptism?," 28.

The Reformed have no problem with the Holy Spirit working faith through means, so long as that means is exclusively preaching, which makes their argument for infant baptism tenuous at best. In his commentary on the Heidelberg Catechism, Thelemann writes, "The Holy Ghost makes use of both Word and Sacraments, the former to work faith in our hearts, the latter to confirm faith in our hearts.[211] Godfrey adds that in the sacraments, God presents his Word to us in tangible form. He writes, "It is the same Word, but in a different form, a form that particularly speaks to our senses."[212] If it is the same Word, why subordinate the sacramental Word to the preached Word? This bifurcation of the Word is unnecessary and unfortunate, as Calvinists freely ascribe to preaching regenerative opportunities for the Spirit that are *verboten* to the sacraments. Thus, Sproul argues that regeneration is not caused by "baptism," but is only "signified" by baptism.[213] The Holy Spirit's power to regenerate a sinner is limited to the pulpit alone in Reformed theology.

I invite you to read John 3:5 once more and answer the following question, "According to Jesus, how is one born again?" His words to Nicodemus are not as mysterious as evangelical commentators would lead us to believe. Jesus is simply instituting what had been promised through Ezekiel. When the Messiah came, he was going to sprinkle us with pure water and give us new hearts by putting his Spirit within us (Ezek 36:24–27). Since Jesus sets no limitation on the Holy Spirit making use of water to usher us into his kingdom through spiritual rebirth, neither should we.

Titus 3:4-6

[4]*But when the goodness and loving kindness of God our Savior appeared,* [5]*he saved us, not because of works done by us in righteousness, but according to his own mercy, by the washing of regeneration and renewal of the Holy Spirit,* [6]*whom he poured out on us richly*

---

[211]Thelemann, *Aid to the Heidelberg Catechism*, 244.

[212]Godfrey, "Why Baptism?," 28.

[213]Sproul, *Truths We Confess*, 3:116.

through Jesus Christ our Savior, [7]so that being justified by his grace we might become heirs according to the hope of eternal life.

Paul builds upon the Lord's words to Nicodemus by explicitly linking God's salvation to baptism, regeneration, the Holy Spirit, grace, justification, and eternal life through Jesus Christ. Reu notes the profundity of this passage:

> God saved us, Paul declares, by the apparently trivial means of a bath, a washing; but, he adds, this washing differs from all other applications of water and is absolutely unique and matchless because it mediates the Holy Spirit's gift of regeneration and renewal. Without this regeneration and renewal performed by the Holy Spirit, the application of water would be no means of salvation; it has this saving efficacy because regeneration and renewal are inseparably connected with it.[214]

Paul begins with a simple fact. *God saved us.* He clarifies by excluding humanity's works or cooperation from the equation (*not because of works done by us in righteousness*). What then is our salvation based upon? *God's mercy.* By what means? He saved us *through the washing of regeneration and the renewal of the Holy Spirit, whom he poured out on us richly through Jesus Christ our Savior.*

We have already seen the term "wash" (*louo*) in connection with Paul's own baptism (Acts 22:16). It is a well attested baptismal term employed in the New Testament, which many Reformed commentators accept (i.e. Eph 5:26; 1 Cor 6:11; Heb 10:22). Citing this passage and the next (Eph 5:26), Horton writes, "The sign and thing signified are treated in the New Testament, as in the Old, as intimately connected."[215] He is willing to grant baptism and regeneration an "intimate connection," but not a cause and effect relationship. This is significant because Paul makes it very clear that baptism has an "instrumental connection" to regeneration by the power of the Holy Spirit, especially in light of his use of the genitive case, which demonstrates possession in Greek. The genitive nouns for washing

---

[214]Reu, *Lutheran Dogmatics*, 272.

[215]Horton, *Christian Faith*, 790.

(*loutrou*) and regeneration (*palingenesias*) can be understood in one of the following ways:

- Possessive sense: "wash belonging to regeneration"
- Qualitative sense: "regenerating wash"
- Objective sense: "wash effecting regeneration."

Lenski concludes, "Any one of these genitive translations retains the main point, namely, that this bath and this regeneration plus the renewing are inseparably connected: where the bath is, there the regeneration and the renewing are."[216] Baptism thus receives its power from the Holy Spirit; he is the possessive author. The Spirit, sent by Christ, brings the benefits of Christ with him into the hearts of the baptized as they are born again and justified by his grace through faith. Even Plummer, a non-Lutheran commentator, is forced to come to terms with Paul's text by treating it with admirable honesty:

> We are fully justified by his language here in asserting that it is by means of the baptismal washing that the regeneration takes place; for he asserts that God 'saved us *through* the washing of regeneration.' The laver or bath of regeneration is the instrument or *means* by which God saved us. Such is the natural and almost necessary meaning of the Greek construction (*dia* with the genitive). Nor is this an audacious erection of a comprehensive and momentous doctrine upon the narrow basis of a single preposition. Even if this passage stood alone, it would still be our duty to find a meaning for the Apostle's Greek: and it may be seriously doubted whether any more reasonable meaning than that which is here put forward can be found.[217]

As we have seen, this passage does not stand alone. It is one of many to advance the saving efficacy of this missionary sacrament.

---

[216]Lenski, *Titus*, 933.

[217]Plummer, *Pastoral Epistles*, 288.

Baptism Sanctifies

Ephesians 5:25–27

²⁵*Husbands, love your wives, as Christ loved the church and gave him-self up for her,* ²⁶*that he might sanctify her, having cleansed her by the washing of water with the word,* ²⁷*so that he might present the church to himself in splendor, without spot or wrinkle or any such thing, that she might be holy and without blemish.*

Paul charges husbands to love their wives as Christ loves his church. The motif of God's relationship as a marriage with his people is inter-woven throughout the scriptures. It is likely that Paul is applying the themes of Ezekiel 16:8–14 to Christ as the heavenly bridegroom, who has chosen and washed his bride clean through his baptismal word:

> Then I passed by you and watched you, noticing that you had reached the age for love. I spread my cloak over you and covered your naked-ness. I swore a solemn oath to you and entered into a marriage cove-nant with you, declares the sovereign LORD, and you became mine. Then I bathed you in water, washed the blood off you, and anointed you with fragrant oil. (Ezekiel 16:8–9)[218]

As previously noted, the idea of "washing" in connection with baptism and the new birth is an important dimension of baptism. The revered Scottish Presbyterian, Sinclair Ferguson, is right to hear an echo of Jesus' words to Nicodemus. He writes, "That supernat-ural birth cleanses us. It ordinarily takes place within the context of the proclamation of the gospel."[219] Once more we have a Calvin-ist who advances the new birth through preaching, but completely ignores the fact that Paul includes the *washing of water* in addition to the word. While Lutherans happily affirm the saving power of preaching the Gospel as a means of grace (Rom 10:17), the failure to mention even the possibility of baptism in a popular evangelical

---

[218]Note also the parallel with Gal 3:26–28 (the bride being "clothed" and having her nakedness covered).

[219]Ferguson, *Ephesians*, 154.

commentary on this passage is egregious. Ignoring the text is no way to interpret the text.

The "washing" (*loutro*) in the Greek is dative, expressing the idea of "in," "with," and especially "to." Christ has sanctified and cleansed his church by means of "washing with the water" in connection with the "word" (*en rhemati*). The preposition *en* indicates concomitance, that with which the water is bound. It is unlikely that *en rhemati* is referring to the preached word, but rather, its close association with "cleansing," "water," and "washing" suggest it should be understood as a reference to the baptismal formula (Christ's *rhema* of institution). The *en rhemati* has no article because the water linked with the spoken word is a single concept, further supporting baptism.

Having been cleansed and sanctified by the water and word, we find the eschatological blessings that follow. Christ will present to himself a beautiful bride whom he has made holy and blameless through his appointed means (v. 27). As Jenson remarks, "If the church is described as the bride of Christ, baptism makes it possible to say to those outside: 'You will be virginal in that bath,' and to those inside: 'You have been wedded to the Lord, and cannot love another.'"[220]

Ongoing Significance for the Baptized

We are far from exhausting the many passages and salutary benefits of baptism in the New Testament, but what we have considered thus far should suffice in demonstrating the abundantly clear teaching of Scripture concerning the efficacy of baptism. When one is baptized into the Name of the Triune God, they actually receive new birth (John 3:5), forgiveness of sins (Acts 2:38–39), union with Christ (Rom 6:3–4), sanctification and cleansing (Eph 5:26)—in short, salvation (1 Pet 3:21).

Far from being a spiritual symbol of grace that has little significance for the ongoing discipleship of a believer, baptism is to be used by Christians throughout their life. While the apostles never call for

---

[220]Jenson, *Visible Words*, 145.

rebaptism, they do recall the baptism that has once been received.[221] Luther acknowledges the same when he says that the Christian life is nothing else than a daily baptism, once begun and ever to be continued.[222] Scaer notes baptism's lasting significance:

> Regardless of what may be considered progress in the Christian life, the believer always stands at the beginning of his sojourn and thus is always in need of what his baptism has given. At the frontier between God's and Satan's kingdom, he again and again renounces Satan, confesses faith in the Triune God, and receives everything which baptism offers. Baptism is performed once, but its effect is daily supplied. Those who do not have a life-encompassing concept of baptism suffer as much from a defective anthropology as they do from a defective sacramentology.[223]

It is my opinion that the Reformed not only possess a defective sacramentology, but a defective hermeneutic that is supported, in part, by a fear of God using his external creation to accompany his saving Word. Therefore, I find the Calvinist position on baptism to be purely noetic, which is to say, a sacrament that visibly advertises a gracious God to the intellect, but does not actually deliver the grace signified therein. It is far more satisfying to know that in baptism, Christ is truly present as both the giver of the grace received and the object of faith.

---

[221]See Rom 6:3–13; 1 Cor 1:13; 6:11; 12:13; Eph 4:5; Col 2:12; Tit 3:5–6; 1 Pet 3:21.

[222]Large Catechism IV, 65, *Triglotta*, 743.

[223]Scaer, "Baptism and the Lord's Supper," 42.

The Lord's Supper—Part 1

The Personal Union of the Two Natures in Christ

Some of the most heated controversies during the Reformation centered upon the Lord's Supper. Luther exposed the false doctrine and practice of the medieval church by rejecting the sacrifice of the Mass, the theory of transubstantiation, and withholding the cup from the laity. "But no sooner had Luther cleansed the sacrament from Roman perversions," remarks Bjarne W. Teigen, "than he found the sacrament attacked from another quarter, from those who wanted to spiritualize the sacrament."[224] Calvinism represents one of the more nuanced strains of those who spiritualize the Lord's Supper. According to Alister McGrath, Calvin may be regarded as occupying a middle place between the two extremes represented by Luther and Zwingli, though I find such sentiment be an oversimplification.[225]

Sproul affirms that throughout the history of the church the majority have agreed that Jesus is really present in the Lord's Supper; the point of contention is the *mode* of his presence.[226] Lutherans and Calvinists both speak of Christ's "real presence" in the Supper, but what each tradition means by this phrase is not the same. The foremost issue between our traditions centers upon how Christ's presence is related to the words of institution in Matthew 28:26–28,

---

[224]Teigen, *I Believe: A Study of the Formula of Concord*, 11.

[225]McGrath, *Reformation Thought*, 182.

[226]Sproul, *What is the Lord's Supper*, 32–33.

Mark 14:22–24, Luke 22:14–20, and 1 Corinthians 11:23–26; but by default, it initiates a parallel Christological debate.

Calvin rejected Luther's understanding of the real presence, in part, because he restricted the humanity of Christ to the confines of heaven following his ascension to the right hand of the Father. In his *Consensus Tigurinus* (1549)—a sacramental confession of unity between the reformers of Geneva and Zurich—Calvin placed Luther's understanding of Christ's presence in his crosshairs with this warning:

> We must guard particularly against the idea of any local presence. For while the signs are present in this world, are seen by the eyes and handled by the hands, Christ, regarded as man, must be sought nowhere else than in Heaven, and not otherwise than with the mind and eye of faith. Wherefore it is a perverse and impious superstition to enclose him under the elements of this world.[227]

Based upon the celestial containment of Christ's human nature, Calvin believed that a literal reading of Christ's words, "This is my body; this is my blood," was preposterous and should be interpreted figuratively. Calvin reasoned, "It is the true nature of a body to be contained in space, to have its own dimensions and its own shape."[228] Thus, Sproul concludes that the Reformed tradition rejected Luther's understanding of the Lord's Supper, not on sacramental grounds, but Christological grounds.[229] Since this is one of the crucial points of debate concerning Christ's presence in the Supper, this chapter will present a Lutheran understanding of the incarnation and the personal union of the two natures in Christ in order to remove the false Christological barriers that Geneva has consistently erected to dissuade people from a simple reading of Christ's words of institution. We will begin by considering the theological implications of Christ's session at the right hand of the Father, since Calvin made this a fundamental reason for his dismissal of Luther's position.

---

[227]*Consensus Tigurinus*, Art. 21.

[228]Calvin, *Institutes*, 4.27.29.

[229]Sproul, *What is the Lord's Supper*, 38.

Christ's Session at the Right Hand of the Father

There are numerous scriptural references to Jesus sitting at the right hand of God.[230] Its significance is marked by the fact that both the Apostles' and Nicene Creeds include it in the narrative of the second article. The Bible is clear that God is spirit (John 4:24), and therefore, both Lutherans and Reformed have understood the expression "right hand of God" as anthropomorphic, a metaphor in which the point of comparison is not spatial position, but strength and power.[231] Two primary ideas emerge in the Old Testament:

1. Special favor or status. In the ancient world to be seated at the right hand is to occupy a place of recognition and importance. Solomon's mother was given a throne at the right hand of the king (1 Kgs 2:19). The Messiah is commanded to sit at the right hand of the Lord in Psalm 110:1, a position of honor and glory (cf. Matt 22:44). "In the case of Christ," notes Berkhof, "it was undoubtedly an indication of the fact that the Mediator received the reigns of government over the Church and over the universe, and is made to share in the corresponding glory."[232]

2. The execution of power. God's "right hand" is most often employed for God's power and protection. Thus, Moses sings, "Your right hand, O Lord, was majestic in power, your right hand, O Lord, shattered the enemy" (Exod 15:6). Jesus is pictured in Revelation as One enthroned beside the Father, crowned with glory and honor on account of the great victory he gained over sin and death, through obedience to his Father's will (Rev 4–5).

The question during the Reformation debates remains important, "Where is the Father's right hand?" Luther argued against Zwingli

---

[230]Matt 26:64; Mark 14:62; Luke 22:69; Acts 2:33; Eph 1:20; Col 3:1; 1 Pet 3:22; Heb 8:1, 12:2.

[231]See Schaller, *Biblical Christology*, 110–114.

[232]Berkhof, *Systematic Theology*, 352.

that the right hand of the Father is not a place, as though "Christ has no other glory than to sit at the right hand of God on a velvet cushion and let the angels sing and fiddle and ring bells and play before him, and to be unconcerned with the problem of the Supper."[233] Zwingli and Calvin assumed that God is far removed from his creation. But for Luther, since God is everywhere present, his right hand must also be everywhere present.

Lutherans do not deny the existence of a heavenly realm, but simply affirm with the Chronicler that the heavens—even the highest of heavens—cannot contain God (2 Chr 6:18). In the New Testament, Heaven most commonly refers to the abode of God, the angels, and the departed saints. In keeping with biblical usage heaven is contrasted not only with earth but with the universe, the sense being that Christ has entered into an exalted state of being; not only have the "heavens received him" (Acts 3:21), but he "ascended far above all the heavens that he might fill all things" (Eph 4:8–10). The Bible never speaks of heaven as a place far, far away; in fact, it is not a material place that can be measured in terms of miles, kilometers, or even light-years from earth.

In a sermon celebrating the Ascension of our Lord, Norman Nagel makes an acute observation concerning the cloud that took Jesus out of the disciple's sight when he ascended (Acts 1:9). This was no ordinary cloud, and in fact, this cloud is found throughout the Bible as the visible manifestation of God's abiding presence, often referred to as the *Shekinah*: Israel was led out of Egypt by a pillar of cloud by day (Exod 13:21–22); God spoke out of the same cloud to Moses, assuring him that his presence would remain (Exod 33:9); the cloud filled Solomon's Temple with its glory (1 Kgs 8:10–13); and of course, this cloud was present during Christ's transfiguration (Matt 17:5). As Nagel further elaborates:

> That cloud was a guarantee of the presence of God. So at the ascension a cloud is used to mark Jesus' entry to the realm of God, which we can neither understand nor measure with our present little thoughts and limited experience. We can't push our little measuring tapes into that

---

[233]Luther, "This is My Body," AE 37:55, 70.

cloud and say how things have to go on there. They go on as God says, and that is the way with Jesus now. Jesus didn't travel thousands of miles like a space rocket. He rose up a little way above the earth and a cloud received him out of their sight. All that was gone was the sight of Jesus. The cloud means that he is no longer within our ordinary limits. Jesus is now present and does things in the whole range of God's way of being present and doing things while remaining a man, but a man fulfilled and glorified.[234]

On account of the personal union of the two natures in Christ, his bodily resurrection and subsequent exaltation to the right hand of the Father from which he executes his reign as King, the various modes of presence for him transcend what is humanly possible for you and me. This is not a denial, confusion, or the deification of his human nature, as Sproul alleges, but an affirmation of his unique status as the exalted God-man.

We do not pretend to know how Christ is present in the Supper, but believe that he is so as he clearly promised. Without getting mired in metaphysical speculation, Luther spoke of three modes of Christ's presence from Scripture, while acknowledging that he may yet possess other modes that remain unknown to us:

1. Comprehensible (bodily). This is the mode of Christ's presence from the time of his conception until his death when he ministered bodily upon earth. This mode he can still use whenever he wills, as he did following the resurrection, and will use at the last day (Col 3:4).
2. Definitive (illocal). In this mode, Christ neither occupies nor vacates space, but passes through creation as he so desires. For example, this mode was used when he disappeared from the presence of the Emmaus disciples (Luke 24:31) and when he passed through the locked doors of the upper room (John 20:19, 26). Luther sometimes uses the term "spiritual" or "incomprehensible" for this mode, which can be confusing, as Luther did not

---

[234]Nagel, *Selected Sermons*, 145.

employ the word in the same fashion as the Reformed to denote Christ's physical absence from earth or the Supper; but rather, to speak of a supernatural, sacramental mode of his presence accompanying the bread and wine.

A repeated charge against the Lutheran position is that we are "ubiquitists" when it comes to the omnipresence of Christ's human nature.[235] Wilbert Gawrisch observes that the Reformed have consistently misrepresented Lutheran teaching as if it involves a physical or corporeal extension of Christ's body throughout heaven and earth."[236] Schaller responds:

> Lutheran theology generally avoids the term ubiquity, as being altogether inadequate and subject to serious misconception in this connection, because it implies consideration of time and space, of which divine omnipresence is the absolute negation. The presence of Christ's human nature in the universe is not physical, not a diffusion nor an expansion of his body, but precisely that *illocal* presence which belongs to the absolute perfection of God.[237]

The problem with the charge of ubiquity is that it is patently false. Lutherans have repeatedly made this clear in their writings since the sixteenth century. The real presence of Christ in the Supper is not earthly, physical, or Capernaitic (i.e., cannabilistic), but it is true and essential nevertheless, as the words of his testament read, "This is my body."[238]

3.   Divine (repletive). Here we speak of the Son together with the Father and Holy Spirit as one God, whereby he cannot be measured or circumscribed. God fills heaven and

---

[235]See Mathison, *Given for You*, 256–259.

[236]Gawrisch, "On Christology, Brenz, and the Question of Ubiquity," *No Other Gospel*, 243.

[237]Schaller, *Biblical Christology*, 72.

[238]Formula of Concord, Epitome, VIII, 17, *Triglotta*, 823.

earth with his presence without being contained by them or dissolving them into himself. Of this mode of presence, we can say with Luther, "Nothing is so small, but that God is still smaller; nothing is so big, but that God is bigger; nothing is so long, but that God is longer; nothing is so broad, but that God is still broader; nothing is so narrow, but that God is still narrower; and so on."[239]

Such an exalted state of being does not resign Christ, as Calvin asserts, to the spatial limitations of an earthly king. More importantly, we are not here concerned with the mere possibilities of Christ's presence, but explicitly with where he has told us to seek him, as Luther stressed:

> Even though he is present everywhere, he does not let you take hold of him or catch him. He can divest himself of his shell, so that you get the shell and do not take hold of the kernel. Why? Because it is one thing when God is there and another when his is there for you. But he is there for you when he adds his word, binds himself with it, and says: "Here you shall find me." Now when you have the word, you can with assurance take hold of him and have him and say, "Here I have you, just as you say."[240]

The Personal Union of the Two Natures in Christ

1 Timothy 3:16 (ESV)

Great indeed, we confess, is the mystery of godliness: He was manifested in the flesh, vindicated by the Spirit, seen by angels, proclaimed among the nations, believed on in the world, taken up in glory.

Lutherans confess the Christology of Nicea (325 A.D.) that asserts Jesus Christ is one person with a divine and human nature, and both entire. Furthermore, we adhere to the Chalcedonian definition (451 A.D.), affirming the human and divine natures are joined

---

[239]Luther, *Confession Concerning Christ's Supper*, LW, 37:228.

[240]Luther, *This is My Body*, LW, 37:68.

together in the one person of Christ without confusion, change, division, or separation. This orthodox Christological position protects the integrity of both natures while maintaining the unity of Christ's person. The incarnation is an incredible mystery, as Paul writes, whose depth we shall never truly plumb. Since this mystery transcends human reason, it must be received in faith and understood by what has been revealed in Scripture alone.

Written to counter the influence of Calvinism in German territories, the Saxon Visitation Articles of 1592 summarize the Lutheran position on the "person of Christ" in four succinct statements:

1. There are two distinct natures in Christ (divine and human). These remain for eternity and will never be confused or separated.
2. These two natures are personally united with each other in such a way that there is only one person, Jesus Christ.
3. On account of this personal union, it is correctly said—and it is so in fact and truth—that God is man, and man is God, that Mary gave birth to the Son of God (Gal 4:4), and that God redeemed us through his own blood (Acts 20:28).
4. Through this personal union and subsequent exaltation, Christ has been placed at God's right hand according to his human nature and has received all power in heaven and on earth (Matt 28:19), and shares in all divine majesty, honor, power, and glory (Matt 5:31).[241]

The difficult question concerning this personal union follows, "How do the two distinct natures of the one person function if each nature has its own essential attributes, given that these attributes are mutually exclusive?" For example, God is omniscient, while the human brain is limited in how much it can know. God is omnipresent, but a human body can only be in one place at a time. God is infinite, humanity finite. Since Jesus is both God and man he must possess all the attributes of God and man. As God, he is infinite and unlimited, but as man he is finite and limited. Yet there is only

---

[241]See my full translation with accompanying biblical citations in the appendix.

one Jesus Christ, who is at one and the same time both infinite and finite. To better understand this paradox, Lutherans have historically divided this doctrine under three classifications (*genera*), each describing a different aspect of how the Bible actually speaks of the personal union.[242]

Thesis 1: The Attributes of each
Nature are Ascribed to the Whole Person

The unique properties of the two natures are ascribed in the Bible to the whole person of Jesus Christ. Wessel offers a helpful comparison between the union of soul and body in a person to clarify this:

> Thinking is an essential property of the soul; still one does not say, "My soul thinks," but "I think." To be hungry is an essential property of the body; but one does not say, "My body is hungry," but "I am hungry." In both cases the subject is "I," which pronoun designates the *whole person*.[243]

Similarly, the entire person of Jesus can be described with any of his attributes, and often the writers do so according to one nature, while naming him with the attributes of the other. For example, Paul writes the rulers of this world "crucified the Lord of glory" (1 Cor 2:8). Lord of glory is a divine title, and according to his divine nature he cannot die—as death is a property of his human nature. But by virtue of the personal union, Paul is correct to say the Lord of glory was crucified. Thus, we can also say the following, "Mary is the mother of God (*Theotokos*)," or reciprocally, "The Son of God was born of a woman" (Gal 4:4). In Romans 9:5, Paul extols Jesus'

---

[242]The classifications for the communication of attributes or *communicatio idiomatum*, as they are known, can be intimidating for those unaccustomed to reading more advanced works of theology. These three classes go by their Latin names: (1) *genus idiomaticum*, (2) *genus maiestaticum*, and (3) *genus apotelesmaticum*. For those who desire to dig deeper, the gold standard for Lutheranism is *The Two Natures in Christ* by Martin Chemnitz. I have rearranged the order and spelled them out in thesis statements for ease of understanding.

[243]Wessel, *Proof Texts of the Catechism*, 1:161.

Hebrew ancestry while simultaneously proclaiming him "God over all, blessed forever." Understanding the manner in which the Bible speaks of Christ helps us maintain the unity of his person and the enduring distinction of the two natures.

Thesis 2: Both Natures of Christ Participate Together in His Redemptive Work

To redeem the world through his office as our Prophet, Priest, and King, Jesus acts not through one nature alone, but through both natures—each providing its own essential attributes in communion with the other for our salvation. "For there is one God, and there is one mediator between God and men, the man Christ Jesus, who gave himself as a ransom for all" (1 Tim 2:4–5). Christ had to be one person to ensure that each nature would be personally united with the other, thus uniting the work of both natures. Otherwise, how could he shed his blood as man and offer infinite atonement as God, and do both as one single satisfactory offering for all?

According to the apostle John, the "blood of Jesus his Son cleanses us from all sin" (1 John 1:7). In warning the pastors of Ephesus, Paul says the church was obtained with the blood of God's own Son (Acts 20:28). If it were the blood of a mere man, then it could not even cleanse himself, much less all humanity. If he had been two persons, the natures could not have joined in one act but as two. Additionally, if the two natures had been confused or separated, he would have been less than God or more than man. If he had been less than God, he could not have offered sufficient atonement to an infinite and holy God; if he had been more than man, he could not have properly represented humanity as the second Adam. But he is the perfect God-man, so joining the two natures in his person as the Lamb of God who takes away the sin of the world. "Therefore he had to be made like his brothers and sisters in every respect, so that he could become a merciful and faithful high priest in things relating to God, to make atonement for the sins of the people" (Heb 2:17). As Luther put it, "The Person is eternal and infinite, and even one little drop of his blood would have been enough to save the entire world."[244]

---

[244]Cited in Plass, *What Luther Says*, 195.

In his love for us, Christ voluntarily chose to restrain the use of his divine attributes during his earthly ministry in order to carry out the work of our redemption. Paul said that Christ humbled himself by becoming obedient to the point of death, even death on a cross" (Phil 2:8). Why was this necessary? Mueller answers:

> If he had fully used his divine power, he would not have been able to die. If his glory had always been manifest as it was at his transfiguration, the people would not have condemned him. If he had done miracles at every opportunity, they would have saved his life—if only to exploit that power. Instead, he became a servant, not using his divine attributes constantly or fully. Because of this, we are redeemed.[245]

Thesis 3: Divine Attributes are Communicated to Christ's Human Nature

How does the human nature of Christ relate to divine attributes like omnipotence, omniscience, or omnipresence? The answer to this question forms the very crux of the debate on Christ's sacramental presence.

"The Word became flesh and dwelt among us" (John 1:14a). The divine nature was not partially present or limited in any way. The divine and human natures are so closely united in the person of Jesus that wherever one nature is found, so also the other; and whatever one nature does, so also the other participates in doing. Lutherans conclude that the Son of God, after his incarnation, is always and everywhere incarnate (*ensarkos*) with no reserve of the divine nature left over in heaven separated or absent from the body.[246] To say otherwise is to rend the person of Christ, thereby creating two persons. When John states that the "Word became flesh," he is saying that the eternally existing *Logos* (the second person of the Trinity) assumed a human nature consisting of body and soul. The human nature did not become divine, but remains truly human; the divine nature was not weakened, nor did it lose any of its essential properties, but remains truly divine. Of the enfleshed Word, John concludes, "We saw his glory—the glory

---

[245]Mueller, *Believe, Teach, and Confess*, 197.

[246]Pieper, *Christian Dogmatics*, 2:124.

of the one and only, full of grace and truth, who came from the Father"
(John 1:14b). Luther strongly defended Chalcedonian Christology
when it came to Christ's indivisibility:

> Wherever this person is, it is the single, indivisible person, and if you
> can say, "Here is God," then you must also say, "Christ the man is
> present too." And if you could show me one place where God is and
> not the man, then the person is already divided and I could at once
> say truthfully, "Here is God who is not man and has never become
> man." But no God like that for me! For it would follow from this that
> space and place had separated the two natures from one another and
> thus had divided the person, even though death and all the devils
> had been unable to separate and tear them apart. This would leave
> me a poor sort of Christ, if he were present only at one single place,
> as a divine and human person, and if at all other places he had to be
> nothing more than a mere isolated God and divine person without
> the humanity.[247]

Calvin assumed that the human nature could not share in the
attributes of the divine nature, rationalizing that it was impossible
for the body and blood of Christ to truly be present with the bread
and wine in the Sacrament:

> For though philosophically speaking there is no place above the skies,
> yet as the body of Christ, bearing the nature and mode of a human
> body, is finite and is contained in Heaven as its place, it is necessarily
> as distant from us in point of space as Heaven is from Earth.[248]

Calvin's view is that after the incarnation, Christ was not and
is not totally incarnate—that is to say, his human nature is limited
in time and space, both on earth and in heaven, because it is impossible for the attribute of omnipresence, along with all other divine

---

[247]Luther, *Confession Concerning Christ's Supper*, LW, 37:218–219, cited in
Formula of Concord, Solid Declaration, VIII, 82–84.

[248]*Consensus Tigurinus*, Art. 25. The Heidelberg Catechism (Q. 47) simpli-
fies the same, "Christ is true man and true God. As a man he is no longer on
earth."

attributes, to be communicated to the humanity of Christ. Calvin writes that although the whole of Christ is everywhere, still the whole of that which is in him is not everywhere.[249] The eternal Son of God, according to Calvin, rules the universe from a position outside of the man Jesus Christ. This has been called the *extra Calvinisticum*, which the Heidelberg Catechism affirms:

> For since divinity is incomprehensible and everywhere present, it must follow that the divinity is indeed *beyond the bounds of the humanity* which he assumed, and is none the less ever in that humanity as well, and remains personally united to it.[250]

The basis for Calvin's position is derived from his magisterial use of reason and the philosophical maxim, "the finite cannot comprehend the infinite" (*finitum non capax infiniti*), which Zwingli also held.[251] While this may sound logical, the gospel-plus-reason approach of the Reformed tradition runs contrary to the New Testament. As Rudyard Kipling once lamented the gulf between British and Indian cultures, so we can say of the personal union of the two natures in Reformed theology, "Oh, East is East, and West is West, and never the twain shall meet."

The Finite Cannot Contain the Infinite?

Colossians 2:8–10 (ESV)

See to it that no one takes you captive by philosophy and empty deceit, according to human tradition, according to the elemental spirits of the world, and not according to Christ. ⁹For in him the whole fullness of deity dwells bodily, ¹⁰and you have been filled in him, who is the head of all rule and authority.

---

[249]Calvin, *Institutes*, 4.27.30. So also Sproul, *Truths We Confess*, 1:246–47.

[250]Heidelberg Catechism, Q. 48, emphasis mine.

[251]See Sproul, *The Lord's Supper*, 47.

Paul warns the church at Colossae to be on high alert against setting human reason, tradition, and philosophy over and against the truth of Christ. While the specific source of this "philosophy" is debated, Paul clearly believed it challenged the all-sufficient, comprehensive person and work of Christ.[252] The finite cannot comprehend the infinite? "Think again," says Paul. *For in him all the fullness of deity dwells bodily*. In one sentence, Paul confirms that Christ's finite body does in fact contain all the fullness of his infinite divine nature:

- In the person of Jesus Christ the deity dwells bodily.
- Not just a portion of deity, but the "fullness" of it.
- And not only some of the fullness, but "all the fullness" (*pas to pleroma*).
- And not for a limited earthly time, but perpetually, as indicated by the present tense of "dwells" (*katoikei*), since Paul was writing long after the ascension.
- And lastly, this dwelling takes place explicitly in Christ's human body (*somatikos*).[253]

Sproul counters that a six-ounce glass cannot hold an infinite amount of water, concluding that the human nature of Christ cannot hold an infinite God.[254] The trouble with this illustration is that it assumes the incarnate God is bound by the laws of nature. Elsewhere, Sproul has written that nature's laws are God's laws, and as such, they do not operate independently from him.[255] In other words, nature is always subject to its creator, which is why orthodoxy has always affirmed the supernatural and miraculous, especially when it comes to Jesus Christ. Lutherans believe the incarnation is supernatural and unique. There has only been one blessed virgin in the history of humanity to conceive and bear the Son of God.

---

[252]For more on the Colossian heresy, see Capes, Reeves, and Richards, *Rediscovering Paul*, 215–25.

[253]I am indebted to Gawrisch's commentary, "The Practical Application of the Doctrine of the Two Natures of Christ," 6.

[254]Sproul, *What is the Lord's Supper?*, 47.

[255]Sproul, *Invisible Hand*, 188.

Reformed scholars reject the Lutheran position, because they believe it makes the divine nature corporeal or deifies Christ's humanity, but this has never been our understanding.[256] We do not believe in a transformation of the *Logos* into humanity, but rather, the most intimate association of the two natures working in concert to carry out the Father's will. Hoeneke offers a better comparison, "The human soul has the most intimate association with the body, even though it does not become corporeal."[257] So it is with the two natures in the one person.

Following the early church fathers, the Formula of Concord illustrates the *genus maestaticum* with the analogy of iron and fire. An essential attribute of iron is that it is heavy; of fire, that it is hot. Iron in itself is not hot, nor is fire heavy, but intimately join the two by putting an iron rod into a fire, and we have a communication of the fire's attributes to the iron. Thus, we can properly say the iron is both "hot" and "heavy." The essential attribute of the fire—its heat— is assumed by the iron, yet both maintain their distinct attributes as iron and fire without confusion. Moreover, this personal union is not merely a figure of speech as you can see the iron glowing red, and if you were to touch it, you would certainly be burned.[258] Thus, it is a real communication. While no analogy is perfect—especially when comparing it to the incomprehensible wonder of the incarnation—it aids in understanding the truth that in Christ the divine attributes like omnipotence, omniscience, or omnipresence can be conveyed to his human nature without confusing or destroying the uniqueness of either nature. Commenting on Colossians 2:9, Krauth notes:

> If all the fullness of the Godhead in the second person of the Trin-
> ity dwells in Christ bodily, then there is no fullness of that Godhead
> where it is not so dwelling in Christ; and as the human in Christ cannot

---

[256]See the Second Helvetic Confession XI; so also Berkhof, *Systematic Theology*, 324.

[257]Hoeneke, *Evangelical Lutheran Dogmatics*, 3:80. Berkhof acknowledges there are useful points of similarity in the comparison with the union of body and soul in man, *Systematic Theology*, 325.

[258]Formula of Concord, Solid Declaration, VIII, 19, *Triglotta*, 1021.

limit the divine, which is essentially, and of necessity, omnipresent, the divine in Christ must exalt the human. The Godhead of Christ is everywhere present, and wherever present, dwells in the human personally, and, therefore, of necessity renders it present with itself.[259]

Lastly, the communication of majesty (*genus maestaticum*) runs in one direction—from the divine nature to the human nature. Like many Calvinists before him, Mathison believes the Lutheran position is completely arbitrary, insisting that the communication of natures must logically be reciprocal.[260] We reject Reformed reciprocity as we do not derive our theology from logic but the Bible alone. The well-known axiom of the early church is affirmed in our confession, "What Holy Scripture testifies that Christ received in time, he received, not according to the divine nature (according to which he has everything from eternity), but the Person has received it in time, by way and with respect, to the human nature."[261] Simply put, "Nothing can be added to God's divine perfection."[262] Christ is already complete and perfect, since "all the fullness of the Godhead dwells in him bodily." While the apostle Paul provides a comprehensive theological statement of fact, let us consider two specific examples of the *genus maestaticum* at work in the Gospels that demonstrate communication of divine attributes to Christ's human nature.

Example 1: Walking on Water (Omnipotence)

Matthew 14:25–26

As the night was ending, Jesus came to them walking on the sea. [26]*When the disciples saw him walking on the water they were terrified and said, "It's a ghost!" and cried out with fear.*

---

[259]Krauth, *Conservative Reformation*, 507.

[260]Mathison, *Given for You*, 258. The Reformed refer to this as the *genus tapeinotikon*.

[261]Formula of Concord, Solid Declaration, VIII, 57, *Triglotta*, 1035. See also, Pieper, *Christian Dogmatics*, 3:158.

[262]Mueller, *Believe, Teach, and Confess*, 195.

Sproul has rightly said that Christianity is a faith based upon and rooted in miracles. Reformed theology has historically defined miracles as "those supernatural acts performed in the external, perceivable world by the immediate power of God, producing supernatural and extraordinary effects that only God can do."[263] This is often expressed in shorthand as a work that goes against the normal laws of nature (*contra naturam*). Berkhof adds, "If God in the performance of a miracle did sometimes utilize forces that were present in nature, he used them in a way that was out of the ordinary, to produce unexpected results, and it was exactly this that constituted the miracle."[264] I belabor the point because the four Gospels permit no doubt whatsoever that Christ's human nature, even before his exaltation to the right hand of the Father, participated in divine attributes (though not essentially) as many miracle stories testify. Walking on water is just one example.

When Jesus came to the disciples' rescue on the Sea of Galilee, they had been struggling for many hours against the wind and waves. To their surprise, Jesus came "walking on the sea." Morris comments, "They could not envisage any mortal doing what Jesus was doing, so they gave their verdict, *'It's a ghost! What else?"*[265] There is no question that walking on water qualifies as a work that goes against the normal laws of nature, since the human body cannot violate gravity on its own accord. Reformed commentator, Hendriksen, acknowledges, "For him [Christ] the very "laws of nature" are means for the effectuation of his purpose. The winds cannot overturn him. Are they not his willing messengers? The waves cannot drown him. Are they not his obedient servants?[266]"

It is one thing to say that Jesus has the omnipotent power of his divine nature to rebuke the wind and sea by his mere word as he does in an earlier miracle story (Matt 8:27), but here, he clearly communicates to his human nature the ability to walk upon the stormy sea. Both natures share in this very external and perceivable miracle.

---

[263]Sproul, *Invisible Hand*, 188.

[264]Berkhof, *Systematic Theology*, 176.

[265]Morris, *Matthew*, 382.

[266]Hendriksen, *Matthew*, 600.

Calvin offers an alternative explanation in order to protect Christ's humanity from his divinity. He posits that the water by the secret power of God miraculously turned to something like solid pavement, providing Christ with a path to walk upon, which then would keep his humanity from doing anything miraculous.[267] While plausible, Calvin's interpretation seems forced and unnecessary. When Peter courageously stepped out of the boat in faith at Jesus' bidding, we get no sense that he perceived a solid surface; and he most certainly did not find one under his feet when doubt crept in. Matthew says he began to sink and cried out, "Lord, save me!" His sinking beneath the water provides support that the miracle is not found in the sea turning solid, but rather, in the omnipotent manipulation of the body to stay afloat atop the tumultuous water. Matthew concludes his account appropriately. Those who were in the boat worshiped Jesus, saying, "Truly you are the Son of God" (Matt 14:33).

Example 2: The Upper Room Entrance (Omnipresence)

John 20:19

On the evening of that day, the first day of the week, the disciples had gathered together and locked the doors of the place because they were afraid of the Jewish leaders. Jesus came and stood among them and said to them, "Peace be with you."

Even after the disciples saw the empty tomb and heard the reports of Jesus' appearance to the women, they were still weak in faith and fearful of being arrested by the Jewish authorities. John twice mentions the doors being shut or locked (cf. v. 27). First century homes were equipped with doors that had a heavy bolt that could be slid through rings attached to the door and its frame to prevent anyone from entering. The Greek term John uses can mean "shut," but as Morris argues, "locked" is a better translation due to the anxious nature of their gathering.

---

[267]Calvin, *Institutes*, 4.17.29; *Commentaries*, 16:241.

The disciples were afraid (understandably), and they took their pre-
cautions. Now Jesus came and stood among them. This appears to
mean that he had not come through the normal fashion (else what is
the point of mentioning the shut door?). It has been suggested that
Jesus came right through the closed door, or that the door opened
of its own accord or the like. But since Scripture says nothing of the
mode of Jesus' entry into the room, we do well not to attempt to
describe it closely. We can scarcely say more than that the risen Lord
was not limited by closed doors. Miraculously he stood among them,
but the precise way he did it is not indicated.[268]

While Morris is cautious, he at least concedes the miraculous
nature of his entry. Calvin is unwilling to admit that Christ's body
could pass through wooden doors or suddenly appear in a supernatural manner incommensurate with a human body.[269] He argues
the doors opened by divine power, so that Christ simply walked in
and stood among his disciples.[270] He is willing to grant the divine
nature of Christ to open locked doors, but in no way will he allow
his human nature to share in this miraculous appearance. In other
words, Calvin's Christology will not allow him to accept the text as it
naturally reads. Jesus' unexpected appearance, literally "in the middle of" or "among" (*meson*) the disciples, has led most interpreters to
the conclusion that the doors remained shut and locked, given that
John emphasizes this by noting it twice.

In Luke's parallel account, we find the disciples terrified for a
second time, believing they have seen a ghost (Luke 24:37). This helps
explain why Jesus' first action is to show them his visible wounds as
evidence that it is really him. His body can be seen and touched, and
yet, he can also supernaturally enter a locked room. The point here
is to simply acknowledge, contra Calvin, that the resurrected Lord
was not limited by space and time. This is an example of the "illocal"
mode of presence previously mentioned. By virtue of the personal

---

[268]Morris, *John*, 745.

[269]See *Commentaries*, 18:264, where he considers such an interpretation a
"childish trifling" leading to many absurdities (such as Christ's real presence in
the Supper).

[270]Calvin, *Institutes*, 4.17.29.

union, his body is capable of doing what ours is not. That which space and time bound was raised to life eternal and given all authority in heaven and earth (Matt 28:18). A Lutheran understanding of the incarnation is confessing nothing more nor less than Thomas in this account. Jesus is truly Lord and God (John 20:28).

Those who deny the real presence of Christ in the Supper do so because of an incorrect understanding of the person of Christ, which leads them to retranslate or reinterpret Christ's words of institution. Our tradition refuses to subject the incarnate and ascended King of glory to human limitations. While reason may fail to fully comprehend this divine mystery, the acid test of our Christology rests upon this question, "Will we trust the words of Holy Scripture?"

ROUND 6

The Lord's Supper—Part II

Christ's Promise, Presence, and Pardon

In each sacrament there is a divine promise expressed in the Word which accompanies the sacramental elements. The promissory Word of Christ is what makes the sacrament a sacrament; it is a performative speech act that accomplishes what it says.[271] To the promise is added the outward means which serve as a visible confirmation of the fulfillment of the promise. The Word may be without the visible means, but the means can never be without the Word.

As we turn our attention to the institution of the Lord's Supper in this chapter, we must keep in mind "who" said these words, for if I said them you would take them as a joke or dismiss them as the words of a lunatic. But these are the words of God incarnate. If he wanted to say, "This represents my body," or "this symbolizes my absent blood," he certainly could have. It is not as though the Son of God lacked the ability to communicate his command and promise. Moreover, the inspired writers of the New Testament honestly reported what they saw, heard, or had passed down to them by credible witnesses. Regarding the Lord's Supper specifically, Paul writes, "For I received *from the Lord* what I also passed on to you" (1 Cor 11:23, emphasis mine).

---

[271]For those interested in the development of *promissio* as a performative word in Luther's thought, see Bayer, *Martin Luther's Theology*, 50–55.

A promise is only as good as the one who makes it. In every Reformation debate concerning the Lord's Supper, Luther consistently drove his opponents back to Christ's word, for Christ alone is authorized and empowered to make good on his promise. "The words are the first thing," Luther says, "for without the words the cup and bread would be nothing. Further, without bread and cup, the body and blood of Christ would not be there."[272]

The Lord Institutes His Supper

Matthew 26:26–28

[26]*While they were eating, Jesus took bread, and after giving thanks he broke it, gave it to his disciples, and said, "Take, eat, this is my body."* [27]*And after taking the cup and giving thanks, he gave it to them, saying, "Drink from it, all of you,* [28]*for this is my blood, the blood of the covenant, that is poured out for many for the forgiveness of sins.*

The Lord's Supper was instituted during the last Passover Jesus would share with his disciples. More importantly, he instituted it within the immediate context of the betrayal (*on the night in which he was betrayed*). Just as his body is about to be handed over and his blood shed by the authorities of this age, he remains the sovereign King; and with the bread and wine as his testament, bequeaths his body and blood to his disciples.[273] "A testament," writes Luther, "is not any promise, but the last irrevocable will of a person who is about to die, in which he leaves his fortunes, determined and ordered, among whom he wants them distributed."[274] Some have questioned the validity of Luther's use of *diatheke* as "testament" from the words of institution, but his reason for doing so is important. The promise Christ made to us in the Supper consummates all of God's covenant promises throughout redemptive history as they find their fulfillment in Christ's death. Most contemporary English

---

[272]Luther, *Confession Concerning Christ's Supper*, LW, 37:264.

[273]For the importance of the betrayal context, see Forde, "The Lord's Supper as the Testament of Jesus," 5–9.

[274]Luther, *Treatise on the New Testament*, LW, 35:84.

versions of the Bible translate *diatheke* as "covenant," but as Robert Kolb observes:

> If the word is understood as covenant, it must be understood as the kind of covenant that is given by the king to his vassals. The king offers; the king imposes. The covenant is his gift to vassals who have no claim on his protection and rule. Christ's Supper is likewise pure gift . . . Thus, it is better to think of it as a last will and testament. Here Jesus bestows all his blessings, the blessings of forgiveness and new life, the blessing of his presence, upon his people.[275]

What happens when the church gathers to "do this in remembrance of me" is the same thing that happened on the night in which Jesus was betrayed. The new testament is distributed to his heirs.

> Rather, the will of Jesus is carried out, the supper *extended now through time* to include all Jesus' heirs in accordance with the will itself. It is not a symbol wrapped up in a ritual time warp, not a repetition, not a representation, not merely a memory, but rather a real event in our time. It is what it says: the new testament.[276]

Linking the Supper to his imminent death, Jesus transforms the Passover of the old covenant into the meal of "the new testament in my blood" (Luke 22:20). In these words Jesus declares to us that the Old Testament Passover has come to its fulfillment in his death upon the cross. He calls the cup the "new testament in his blood," because he is the true Passover Lamb. Art Just notes, "These words imply a new manner of presence of his body and blood distinct from Jesus' normal manner of presence during his earthly ministry, but one that is no less real."[277] According to Jesus, the bread is his body, and the content of the cup (wine) is his blood. There is no grammatical reason to interpret the words of institution other than they plainly read, for Jesus is not employing a parable or metaphor. What Jesus gave

---

[275]Kolb, *Christian Faith*, 228–29.

[276]Forde, "The Lord's Supper as the Testament of Jesus," 8.

[277]Just, *Luke 9:51–24:53*, 826.

the disciples was certainly bread and wine. This is not in dispute. But what he gave them to "take and eat," as well as "drink," was just as certainly more than bread and wine. Luther captures this in his concise definition, "The Sacrament of the Altar is the true body and blood of our Lord Jesus Christ, under the bread and wine, for us Christians to eat and to drink, instituted by Christ himself."[278]

This is My Body: *A Hermeneutical Test Case*

The most contentious words of the institution read: "This is my body" (*Touto estin to soma mou*) and "This is my blood of the covenant" (*Touto gar estin to aima mou tes diatheke*). Since each sentence is simple and similarly constructed, we'll examine the first regarding Christ's body as a hermeneutical test case.

The sentence consists of a subject (this) and a predicate (my body), connected by the copula (is). "This" is a demonstrative pronoun referring to that which Jesus gave to the disciples with the words, "Take, eat." The predicate "my body" denotes the material part of his human nature in contrast to the immaterial (i.e. soul). For example, when Joseph of Arimathea asked Pilate for the "body" of Jesus, there was no confusion concerning his request. Pilate ordered the lifeless body to be given to him (Matt 27:58), thus the women followed and saw where Jesus' body was laid in the tomb (Luke 23:55). The Greek form *to soma mou* is more precise than its English equivalent, as the preceding article, *to*, marks it as the one specific body—visibly and tangibly present before the disciples—as that to which *totou* refers.

Calvin argued that the words of institution are to be understood figuratively by means of metonymy, since the body and blood of Jesus are confined in heaven.[279] But where is the figure of speech located? It cannot be located in the subject, *touto*, for there are no symbolic or metaphorical concepts to be found in the context of

---

[278]Small Catechism, VI, *Triglotta*, 555.

[279]*Consensus Tigurinus*, Art. 22. A metonymy is a figure of speech in which a thing or an idea is called not by its own name, but by the attribute or name of something associated in meaning.

the passage for which *touto* might compare. After all, the bread that Jesus broke and gave the disciples to eat was real bread.

Nor can the figure of speech be found in the copula, *estin*, for it is the job of a linking verb to connect the subject and predicate as a true subject and predicate. Lutherans have provided ample grammatical evidence over the years to defend the fact that "is" means "is" within the context of the Eucharist, but when all is said and done, we are simply confessing that when Christ says, "This is my body," he truly placed the subject, *touto*, and the predicate, *soma mou*, in a real relationship as subject and predicate, and this is supported by the copula, *estin*, following the rules of grammar.[280]

A Reformed pastor and friend recently argued for a figurative interpretation of the Supper by pulling up Google Maps™ on his cell phone, pointing to a dot on the map of Washington state, saying, "This is Seattle."[281] While it sounds clever, context always dictates use. In this case, I clearly understood the figurative use of the predicate as we were literally standing in the middle of downtown Seattle looking at a computerized map on his phone. The subject (this) refers to the digital dot on the map. It is a cartographic representation of the predicate (Seattle), thus the copula (is) equates the two for the purpose of geographic depiction. Clearly the context of a Google Map™ search is very different than the upper room institution on the night of Christ's betrayal, where the predicate of the sentence (my body) was sitting within arm's reach of the disciples.

In Luke's account, we find an important addition, "This is my body, given for you" (Luke 22:19). The body "given" in the Supper and on the cross was no virtual reality; neither was it a symbol of an absent body, nor was it figuratively given. It was his true human body that was nailed to the cross, just as the blood he shed was real human blood. As Krauth asserts, "We believe that the bread is there on the evidence of the senses; we believe that Christ's body is there on the evidence of the Word."[282]

---

[280]For a comprehensive look at the history of grammatical arguments, see Krauth, *Conservative Reformation*, 585–830.

[281]Frame employs a similar argument, *Salvation Belongs to the Lord*, 283.

[282]Krauth, *Conservative Reformation*, 787.

Sproul acknowledges that when something is said "to be" something else, the verb "to be" serves as an equal sign.[283] However, he refuses to accept the sacramental conclusion by shifting his argument away from the words of institution to instances where "to be" verb forms are used metaphorically, where "to be" may mean "represents," leading many Calvinists to retranslate the words of institution to read, "This *represents, symbolizes,* or *signifies* my body."[284]

To defend this grammatical shift, Reformed writers like Sproul point to the "I Am" sayings of Jesus in John's Gospel for support. After all, Jesus did say, "I am the vine; you are the branches" (John 15:5). Is Jesus a literal vine rooted in the soil sprouting leaves and fruit? "Of course not," the Calvinist responds, "Jesus never intended for us to take him literally, and so it is with the words of institution." The context and grammar of the "I am" sayings demonstrate that Jesus is utilizing a figure of speech, because there is a straightforward *tertium comparationis* underlying the metaphor between vine and branches. The preceding verse, "Just as a branch cannot bear fruit by itself, unless it remains in the vine, so neither can you unless you remain in me," connects with the words that follow, "The one who remains in me—and I in him—bears much fruit." The point Jesus is making is quite simple: Christians (branches) only bear good works (fruit) when they abide in him (vine).

While I commend every attempt to interpret scripture with scripture, we must recognize that when comparing the "I am" sayings to the words of institution, we are dealing with apples and oranges. In every one of the "I am" sayings, the figure of speech lies in the predicate, and the point of comparison is plain from the words that precede or follow. Graebner points out, "The *tertium comparationis* in a trope [figure of speech] must be some characteristic, some quality, state, or relationship, inherent in or connected with the person or thing denoted by the word in its real signification."[285] For example, when Jesus calls the Pharisees serpents and a brood of vipers in Matthew 23:33, it is to

---

[283]Sproul, *What is the Lord's Supper,* 32.

[284]For example, Frame, *Salvation Belongs to the Lord,* 283; so also, Berkhof, *Systematic Theology,* 649–650.

[285]Cited by Wessel, *Proof Texts of the Catechism,* 2:131.

illustrate the very real danger inherent in the Pharisees' hypocrisy. Like venomous serpents, their words are poison to the soul. However, when Jesus said, "Take, eat, this is my body," we find no similar point of comparison or hidden symbolic meaning within the context of the passage to justify a figurative reading. Furthermore, we are commanded to eat and drink, which makes eating and drinking the primary actions of the sacrament. Reu humorously points out that "symbols" are studied and comprehended, but not eaten or drunk.[286]

In his book, *Given for You*, Mathison attempts to reclaim Calvin's doctrine of the Lord's Supper for the contemporary era. Many notable Reformed scholars, including Sproul and Horton, have recommended it as a "must read" for anyone desiring to engage this subject. Mathison sets the words of institution within the context of the Passover, but argues for a non-literal reading based upon the figurative words of the traditional Passover liturgy.

> Normally, the Passover liturgy would include the following words: "This is the bread of affliction which our ancestors ate when they came from the land of Egypt." Of course, the Jews did not believe that they were actually eating the very same pieces of bread their ancestors ate on the night of the first Passover. The main point of contact is not between "this bread" and "that bread." Instead, these words point, by means of a figure of speech, to a real participation by the Jews in the act of redemption that their ancestors experienced first hand . . . At the institution of the Lord's Supper, Jesus changed the words of the liturgy. Rather than saying, "This is the bread," he said, "This is my body." In neither case are the words meant to be understood in an absolutely literal manner. This is readily granted in the case of the original words of the Passover liturgy, and it should be granted in the case of the new words of the eucharistic liturgy.[287]

Though one of the few contextual arguments for a figurative reading, there are a number of problems with this approach.[288] We

---

[286]Reu, *Lutheran Dogmatics*, 306.

[287]Mathison, *Given for You*, 211, 242.

[288]I am building here upon Kom's response in his excellent paper, "Honoring the Lord and His Supper," 32.

know a sentence or phrase is to be taken figuratively if the literal meaning is impossible. For example, when Peter likens Christ to a living stone and chief cornerstone (1 Pet 2:4–6), he is employing a common Old Testament metaphor to praise Christ as the foundation of our faith. No one reading Peter's letter would confuse Jesus with a hard, mineral-based substance of creation. Even so it would be improper to say that Christ "represents" a rock. Like the "I am" sayings, the figure of speech is found in the predicate, providing the point of comparison, not the copula. For Christ truly is the foundation upon which the church rests (cf. Matt 7:24).

When the father of a Jewish family held up the bread at Passover, saying, "This is the bread of affliction," no one believed it was the same bread eaten by the Israelites at the time of the Exodus. It too is clearly a figure of speech. The meaning of the phrase, "bread of affliction," bespeaks the bread eaten during a particular time of affliction in Israel's history. The bread didn't cause the affliction. It represents a specific time when everything was bitter, not even eating was enjoyable, so bitter herbs were also included in the meal. When the Jews ate the bread of affliction they recalled the back-breaking days of slavery before God brought them out of Egypt. In the recitation of these words, Mathison says the Jews identified themselves with the historical Exodus. He concludes, "They identified themselves with the people who were actually there and declared their participation in God's act of redemption."[289]

Is this all there is then to the Lord's Supper? Are we simply identifying ourselves with the disciples who were actually there in the upper room declaring our participation in Christ's act of redemption through the recitation of figurative speech? If we interpret Jesus' words as the Jews interpreted the "bread of affliction," as Mathison suggests, we are left with little more than a sophisticated version of Zwingli's bare symbolism, rather than a recovery of Calvin's doctrine. I find little "new" to the "new testament" in Mathison's approach. It bears repeating "who" said these words, for Jesus was not a Jewish father gathered around the family table recalling past events. He was, and remains, the only begotten Son of God instituting the "*new*

---

[289]Mathison, *Given for You*, 242.

testament," providing for the perpetual sustenance of his church and the proclamation of his death until he returns. Stephenson offers a better approach, "The Lord's decision not to recast, rephrase, or refashion what he had instituted in the upper room strongly suggests that he intended the apostles to understand him as having meant what he said and said what he meant."[290]

Sacramental Union

1 Corinthians 10:16

The cup of blessing that we bless, is it not a participation in the blood of Christ? The bread that we break, is it not a participation in the body of Christ?

The apostle Paul was the first to record the words of institution, and thus, he offers the earliest commentary on the subject of the Lord's Supper. The key word for Paul is *koinonia*, which can be translated in English as participation, fellowship, communion, or joint sharing. In reference to the sacramental cup, Lenski calls *koinonia* an actual and a real participation in the blood of Christ (i.e. the blood shed on the cross for the remission of our sins). If either the wine of the cup or the blood of Christ is not real, then a "communion" between them is also not real (i.e. none exists).[291] The point is that Paul understood a real union of the sacramental elements that include both earthly (bread/wine) and heavenly (body/blood) realities. Walther comments:

> Paul is teaching us that the bread is not the body, but bears the body and is united with it in such a way, that the one who partakes of the bread also partakes of the body. Therefore, when the Lord says, "This is My body," the "this" is bread and body together in sacramental union. Why then doesn't the Lord Himself say, "This bread?" Answer: The disciples see that it is bread which the Lord was giving them according to the Passover ordinance. The new instituted by Christ is that He imparts His body at the same time in a mysterious manner.[292]

---

[290]Stephenson, *Lord's Supper*, 62.

[291]Lenski, *1–2 Corinthians*, 409.

[292]Walther, "Warum Sind die Einsetzungsworth," 158.

Luther spoke of this *koinonia* as a sacramental union (*unio sacramentalis*) in order to defend his position from accusations of impanation and a carnal manner of eating: "As nobody sees, touches, eats or chews the Body of Christ in a way as we see and chew visibly other flesh; for what we do to the bread is attributed to the Body of Christ because of the sacramental union between bread and body."[293] When Luther uses the locatives "in, with, and under" to speak of Christ's presence in the Eucharist, he was not advocating a local presence, as if Christ's body was literally baked into the bread, but rather, a definitive presence that safeguards the Pauline sacramental participation of the body and blood from being separated from the bread and wine as the radical reformers taught. Reu provides a terse, but accurate, response to those who question this union:

> If the possibility of the real presence of Christ's body and blood is questioned, we answer that our exalted Lord is omnipresent also according to his human nature and therefore able to offer His body and His blood where, and whenever, He desires to do so. His marvelous power is unlimited. If the dogma of the *unio sacramentalis* is stigmatized as unreasonable or contra-rational, we reply that, measured by this criterion, every mystery of faith would ultimately have to be surrendered . . . If it is objected that bread and wine, being earthly and transitory substances, could not serve as vehicles for the body and blood of Christ, we would refer to the incarnation of Christ as the plainest proof that the finite may comprehend the infinite. If we are told that it is unworthy of God that we orally receive His body and blood, we praise Him who in grace has condescended to our level in order to assure us of our salvation.[294]

As the doctrinal debates intensified during the sixteenth century, so also did the rhetoric. Reformed writers like Peter Martyr Vermigli called his Lutheran opponents bread worshipers, bloodsuckers, ubiquitists, carnivores, and accused the Lutheran church of celebrating a Thyestean feast by baking the Son of God into the bread.

---

[293]Luther and Bucer (Calvin's mentor in Strasbourg) agreed on this point in the Wittenberg Concord of 1536.

[294]Reu, *Two Treatises on the Means of Grace*, 117–118.

Walther offers further clarification, lest contemporary Reformed readers also misunderstand this sacramental union:

> Luther could not have expressed more clearly how he wanted the presence of Christ's body and blood in the Lord's Supper taught than by saying, as he does here, that the body and blood of Christ are in the consecrated elements not locally but definitively. Hence he merely wanted to affirm the "where," that is, the reality of the presence with the exclusion of all spatial forms of existence; just as, for example, man's spirit, an angel, a glorified body, heaven and hell have their "where," or are definitely somewhere without possessing space or extension. To them belongs illocality, even though they are indeed somewhere.[295]

We do not pretend to comprehend this mystery scientifically; we simply take Christ at his word. The sacramental union rests upon the institution of Christ, and not upon the faith or morality of the administering pastor or that of the communicant, nor does the absence of faith in either invalidate it. It depends upon Christ's efficacious word alone. As the Formulators wrote, "It is just like the gospel: whether the godless hearers believe it or not, it nevertheless is and remains the true gospel."[296]

The union of Christ's body and blood with the bread and wine is not a natural union in a local or circumscriptive place, for when we eat the body of Christ in the Eucharist we are not chewing Christ's flesh like a bite of bratwurst. "We term it *sacramental*," says Graebner, "not to explain it, but to describe it as being peculiar to this sacrament, in accordance with and by virtue of the sacramental word, which we believe."[297]

Mathison counters that Lutherans do not take the words of institution any more literally than the Reformed since we insist that the bread remains bread and that Christ's body is present simultaneously

---

[295] Walther, *Select Writings*, 3:18.

[296] Formula of Concord, Solid Declaration, VII, 89, *Triglotta*, 1003.

[297] Cited by Wessel, *Proof Texts of the Catechism*, 2:140.

with the bread.[298] As we have seen, when Christ said, "Take, eat, this is my body," the subject "this" refers to both the bread and the body. Paul's inspired elaboration cannot be clearer when he says that the bread that we break is a participation in Christ's body. Luther explained this grammatically:

> This mode of speaking about diverse beings is one the grammarians call "synecdoche." It is quite common not only in Scripture but also in all languages. For instance, if I point to or hand over a bag or purse and say, "This is a hundred gulden," both the gesture and the word "this" refer to the purse. But since the purse and the money in some degree constitute one object, one lump, my words apply at the same time to the money.[299]

Because Luther uses the term "synecdoche," Mathison argues that Luther advanced a nonliteral reading. While a synecdoche may technically be a figure of speech, it is not figurative speech. The difference is that it does not employ metaphor or a nonliteral figure in order to remove the reality of Christ's body or bread in the sacramental eating and drinking. The sentence, "This is my body," is a synecdoche, because the bread is used to refer to Christ's body, yet the bread that does the containing is not identical with the body it contains, and vice versa. Together they form a unity-in-distinction, with an emphasis on their unity.[300] A basic hermeneutical principle is that the literal meaning of a passage is the one the author or speaker intended to convey. If Jesus used a synecdoche, as Luther believed, then his interpretation of the passage is in fact a literal and truthful reading; and by default, any opposing opinion would, therefore, be in error.

Before moving on, I must address the persistent, yet false, designation of the Lutheran position as "consubstantiation," despite it being refuted repeatedly in many early Lutheran treatises on the Lord's Supper, and confessionally, in the Formula of Concord. For example, in his influential book, *The History of Christian Doctrine,*

---

[298]Mathison, *Given for You*, 259.

[299]Luther, *Confession Concerning Christ's Supper*, LW, 37:301.

[300]Hunsinger, "Bread that We Break," 249.

Berkhof says that Luther substituted transubstantiation for consubstantiation, equating his position on the Lord's Supper with that of William of Ockham.[301] While Mathison acknowledges that Lutherans object to this term, he nevertheless uses it as a subhead to critique Luther's position, ironically stating he could find no pejorative connotations with it.[302] Not pejorative? We deny consubstantiation because it is not what Lutherans believe, teach, and confess. It is a pejorative term because it communicates falsehood. A scholar of Mathison's caliber should know that consubstantiation is an actual historical position on the Lord's Supper with a history of proponents that predate Luther. In his dictionary of theological terminology, Muller accurately defines consubstantiation:

> According to the theory of consubstantiation, the body and blood of Christ become substantially present together with the substance of bread and wine, when the elements are consecrated. The theory is frequently confused with the Lutheran doctrine of real presence. *Consubstantiatio* indicates the presence of Christ's body according to a unique sacramental mode of presence that is proper to Christ's body as such, and is therefore a local presence (*praesentia localis*, q.v.); the Lutheran view, however, argues a real, but illocal presence of Christ's body and blood that is grounded in the omnipresence of Christ's person, and therefore a supernatural and sacramental, rather than a local, union with the visible elements of the sacrament.[303]

If I were to mislabel Calvin's position on the Supper with the subhead, "memorialism," I am certain Calvinists would take similar issue. Why? Because it would be mischaracterizing his doctrinal position, either to purposefully mislead unsuspecting readers to gain rhetorical advantage or through sheer incompetence. Either one would be inexcusable in a book purporting to teach the truth.

---

[301]Berkhof, *History of Christian Doctrine*, 254.

[302]Mathison, *Given for You*, 256.

[303]Muller, *Dictionary of Latin and Greek Theological Terms*, 80. The doctrine of consubstantiation was developed during the Middle Ages and garnered favor with Duns Scotus and William of Okham. Lutherans rejected this concept as it took its bearings from the non-biblical category of "substance."

Calvin and the Spiritual Mode of Christ's Presence

Just as Reformed writers have erroneously mischaracterized the Lutheran position as having no exegetical support by reducing our doctrine of the real presence to a physical, local presence despite confessional statements to the contrary, many Lutherans have returned the favor by failing to notice the subtlety in Calvin's understanding of the real presence that differs from Zwingli. Calvin did believe that Christ's body was present at the Eucharist, but not in the bread or your mouth. Muller notes that Calvin occupies a place between Luther and Zwingli, valuing Luther's stress on Christ's presence, while respecting Zwingli's Christology that maintains the local and physical presence of Christ's body in heaven.[304]

Calvin affirmed the spiritual presence of Christ in the Supper. The bread and wine act as physical symbols to inform believers analogically of the true spiritual realities in which we also partake of according to our union with Christ's divine nature. As Calvin writes, "From the physical things set forth in the Sacrament we are led by a sort of analogy to the spiritual things. Thus, when bread is given as a symbol of Christ's body, we must at once grasp this comparison: as bread nourishes, sustains and keeps the life of our body, so Christ's body is the only food to invigorate and enliven our soul."[305] Calvin's separation from Rome and Luther on this doctrine was over the mode of Christ's presence, not the fact of his presence. For Calvinists, the bread and wine are sacramental symbols that represent the reality of Christ's body and blood that are received in faith, since they are locally present in heaven. The symbols, Hunsinger insists, are not empty. In the act of reception, the bread alone is in the mouth, while the life-giving flesh of Christ, and so Christ in person himself, enters into one's heart by faith.[306] The Westminster Confession captures this distinction:

---

[304]Muller, "Calvin on Sacramental Presence," 147–148, acknowledges both sides have historically struggled to portray each other's position accurately.

[305]Calvin, *Institutes*, 4.17.3.

[306]Hunsinger, "Bread that we Break," 251.

In the sacrament we partake not only outwardly the visible elements, but also inwardly by faith, really and indeed, but not carnally or corporally, but spiritually, receive and feed upon Christ crucified, all the benefits of His death; the body and blood of Christ being then not corporally in, under, or with the bread and wine; but really, as spiritually, present to the faith of believers, as the elements themselves are to the outward senses.[307]

When Jesus said, "This is my body," Calvin interprets this is as a figurative form of expression, in which the Lord gives to the sign the name of the thing signified. Calvin claims that Lutherans improperly apply the body of Christ to the bread in the words of institution, since it is just a sign of it.[308] But how can Christ be truly present in the sacrament if the bread is just a sign of Christ's heavenly body? Calvin answers it is made possible through the power of the Holy Spirit.

Even though it seems unbelievable that Christ's flesh, separated from us by such great distance, penetrates to us, so that it becomes our food, let us remember how far the secret power of the Holy Spirit towers above all our senses, and how foolish it is to wish to measure his immeasurableness by our measure. What, then, our mind does not comprehend, let faith conceive: that the Spirit truly unites things separated by space.[309]

Christ does not descend to us at the table, but rather, by the power of the Holy Spirit the believer mystically ascends to heaven to commune there with Christ. As Calvin states, "For since this mystery is heavenly, there is no need to draw Christ to earth that he may be joined to us."[310] Calvin reverses the traditional catholic sacramental direction of the Supper. The meal acts as a spiritual ladder to take us to heaven.

---

[307]Westminster Confession, XXIX, 7.

[308]Calvin, *Commentaries*, 17:208.

[309]Calvin, *Institutes*, 4.17.32; Geneva Catechism, Q. 354; "Last Admonition to Westphal," SW, 2:416.

[310]Calvin, *Institutes*, 4.17.31.

Let us carefully observe, then, when we wish to use the sacraments as God has ordained, that they should be like ladders, for raising us on high. For we are heavy and cumbersome, held down by earthly things. Thus, because we are unable to fly high enough to draw near to God, he has ordained sacraments for us like ladders. If a man wishes to leap on high, he will break his neck in the attempt; but if he has steps, he is able to proceed with confidence. So also if we are to reach our God, let's use the means which he has instituted for us, since he knows what is suitable for us.[311]

Calvin's position is at least consistent: his Christology, sacramental definitions, and biblical interpretations are uniform throughout his writings, albeit, wrong, for several reasons.

First, there is no mention of the Holy Spirit's role in the biblical passages concerning the Supper. This is not to say that the Spirit, as a member of the Holy Trinity, does not participate in the redemptive benevolence of the sacrament, but to make the Spirit the sole conduit of Christ's presence is to do disservice to the actual text. Paul writes, "The bread that we break is a participation in the body of Christ" (1 Cor 10:16). If Calvin is right, it follows that the bread would not be a sharing of the body of Christ but of the Spirit of Christ, if Christ's body were not truly present but only the Holy Spirit. While Calvin's desire to maintain the Lord's presence is laudable, he is compelled to elevate the Spirit's role due to an inadequate theology of Christ's person. Ultimately, his Christology collapses into Pneumatology to accommodate a kind of sacramental presence that is without scriptural warrant.[312]

Second, the mystical *sursum corda* of believers to heaven via a sacramental ladder in order to receive Christ by faith is an eisegetical insertion that is simply foreign to the scriptural witness. If Jesus is incapable of descending to be present here on earth in the sacrament, how is it that we, who only possess a human nature, are able to ascend into the heavenly court without departing bodily from earth? Where in the four accounts of the Last Supper is this heavenly transportation

---

[311]Cited in Godfrey, "Calvin on the Eucharist," 50.

[312]For the role of the Holy Spirit, see especially Jesus' promises in John 14:16–26, 15:26–27, and 16:7–15.

of believers in the Supper located? We get no sense of a "Lord, beam me up" scenario on the night of Christ's betrayal. Instead, the reality in these passages is one of heaven on earth, Christ adventing, as it were, with his gathered assembly in the *koinonia* of the consecrated bread and wine. The movement of the sacrament is from Christ to the table where he both hosts and feeds us with his body.

Third, Calvin needlessly separates the sign (*signum*) from what it signifies (*res*). Lutherans believe the signs participate in the reality they communicate, which has been the consistent position of the catholic tradition not only in the West, but also the East. Speaking of how the symbol of bread is related to the reality of Christ's body, Alexander Schmemann, an Eastern Orthodox theologian, writes, "The symbol does not so much 'resemble' the reality that it symbolizes as it *participates* in it and therefore it is capable of communicating it in reality."[313]

Fourth, as Pieper points out, Calvin's position on the Lord's Supper requires a great amount of exegesis to explain away what is essentially a very simple text.

> Christ would have had to give approximately this commentary on His words: "True, My words, 'Take, eat; this is My body,' sound as if I were calling on you to eat with your mouth. But don't imagine that My body is here on earth in the Sacrament of the Altar and is intended to be eaten with the mouth (*oralis manducatio*). As distant as heaven is from earth, so far is My body removed from this Supper and your mouth. What I really mean to say with the words, 'Take, eat; this is My body' is this: With the mouth of your faith you are to ascend into heaven and there by faith eat My body spiritually. Furthermore, when I say to you, 'Take, eat; this is My body, which is given for you,' this indeed sounds as though you were receiving that body which is given for you into death and not a symbol or image of My body. However, you must interpret My words according to the axiom that a body always can possess only a local and visible presence and does not extend beyond the natural dimensions of a human body. Since, now, you cannot see My body in My Supper, nor take hold of it with

---

[313]Schmemann, *The Eucharist*, 38.

the hands, you must, when you hear the term "My body," think only of an 'image of My body.'"[314]

Communion of the Unworthy (*Communio Indignorum*)

1 Corinthians 11:27-29 (NRSV)

Whoever, therefore, eats the bread or drinks the cup of the Lord in an unworthy manner will be answerable for the body and blood of the Lord. [28]Examine yourselves, and only then eat of the bread and drink of the cup. [29]For all who eat and drink without discerning the body, eat and drink judgment against themselves.

It should be evident by now that Lutherans possess a dynamic conception of the Lord's Supper. In giving his true body and blood to the communicant, Jesus is bringing the cross to the table for those gathered to eat and drink. From Paul's admonition in 1 Corinthians 11:27–29 we learn that even those who receive the Eucharist without faith partake of the body and blood of Christ, but unto judgment. In other words, Christ's body and blood are present in the sacramental meal regardless of the faith or worthiness of the communicant. Luke observes Judas' presence at the table at the Last Supper, "But look, the hand of the one who betrays me is with me on the table" (Luke 22:21). If our Lord could say to Judas, "Take, eat, this is my body," then the sacramental character of the Supper cannot depend upon the worthiness or faith of the receiver, since Judas the betrayer was certainly not a worthy recipient.[315] The technical term for this is *communio indignorum* (communion of the unworthy).

The chief sin of the Corinthians, according to Paul, was in not properly discerning Christ's body (v. 29) and so treating the sacramental meal like ordinary food and drink. They had made a mockery of the Lord's Supper through class distinctions, drunkenness, and a total disregard for why they had gathered together in the first place, which is why Paul begins, "When you come together, it is not the Lord's Supper you eat" (1 Cor 11:20).

---

[314]Pieper, *Christian Dogmatics*, 3:339.

[315]Krauth, *Conservative Reformation*, 645.

Paul's use of body (*soma*) in verse 27 together with blood (*aima*) reaffirms the real presence and points clearly to the bread/body of the Lord's Supper as being the primary referent of *soma*. For this reason, Paul calls the unworthy communicants "liable" or "guilty" of the body and blood of the Lord. Luther asked the correct interpretive question for those doubting Christ's true presence, "How can you sin in eating the body of the Lord, if he is not present in the eating or the bread?"[316] On account of Christ's real presence, Paul can exhort them to self-examination prior to eating and drinking in verse 28, so that those communing together with the Lord as Christ's body may properly understand what they are receiving and why they are receiving it.

Faith does not cause Christ to be present; rather, it recognizes and receives him.[317] The same sacramental axiom applies to the Lord's Supper as it does in Baptism, "not the sacrament detached from faith, but faith united with the sacrament justifies." How is the Lord's Supper received in a worthy manner? Luther answers:

> Fasting and bodily preparation is, indeed, a fine outward training; but he is truly worthy and well prepared who has faith in these words: *Given, and shed for you, for the remission of sins*. But he that does not believe these words, or doubts, is unworthy and unfit; for the words *for you* require altogether believing hearts.[318]

There are two kinds of eating or partaking in the Lord's Supper, namely, the oral eating and the spiritual eating by faith. The Formula of Concord treats this at length:

> There is, therefore, a twofold eating of the flesh of Christ, one *spiritual*, of which Christ treats especially in John 6:54, which occurs in no other way than with the Spirit and faith, in the preaching and meditation of the Gospel, as well as in the Lord's Supper, and by itself is useful and salutary, and necessary at all times for salvation to all Christians; without

---

[316]Luther, *Against the Heavenly Prophets*, LW, 40:183.

[317]Mueller, *We Believe, Teach, and Confess*, 355.

[318]Small Catechism, VI, *Triglotta*, 557.

which spiritual participation also the sacramental or oral eating in the Supper is not only not salutary, but even injurious and damning . . .

The other eating of the body of Christ is *oral* or *sacramental*, when the true, essential body and blood of Christ are also orally received and partaken of in the Holy Supper, by all who eat and drink the consecrated bread and wine in the Supper—by the believing as a certain pledge and assurance that their sins are surely forgiven them, and Christ dwells and is efficacious in them, but by the unbelieving for their judgment and condemnation, as the words of the institution by Christ expressly declare, when at the table and during the Supper He offers His disciples natural bread and natural wine, which He calls His true body and true blood, at the same time saying: *Eat* and *drink*.[319]

The Reformed reject this two-fold eating, as well as the *communio indignorum*. When Calvin discusses the presence of Christ's body in the Eucharist, he means the efficacy, virtue, power, merit, grace, and spirit of the humanity of Christ. The spiritual eating he espouses—drawn almost exclusively from the "bread of life" discourse in John 6—is simply a participation in the benefits of Christ's body by faith alone, but in no way will he accept a sacramental presence where it is possible for an unworthy communicant to receive Christ's true body and blood. The unbeliever and unworthy receive only bread and wine.

Calvin did, however, maintain that Christ's body was exhibited or offered, but not objectively present to be received by all, like a gift given, but subjectively rejected by those without faith. As he puts it, "it is one thing to be offered, another to be received."[320] Logically, if the Holy Spirit is the sole conduit of Christ's presence in the hearts of believers, as Calvin insists, then it is impossible for Christ to be present for those without the Spirit.

When I've heard this doctrine debated, the question often put forward by the Lutheran side has been, "Is Christ's body objectively present in the sacrament?" This is problematic because "objective" can be ambiguous and is not always afforded the same meaning by both sides. But if we define "objectively present," as Cary suggests,

---

[319]Formula of Concord, Solid Declaration, VII, *Triglotta*, 995.

[320]Calvin, *Institutes*, 4.17.33.

as meaning "present independent of anyone's state of mind," where state of mind includes things like faith, then Christ's body is objectively present in the Lutheran view, but not in Calvin's view. Cary offers a helpful domestic illustration to clarify this distinction:

> I may believe there is no bread in the house, but be mistaken: my wife has bought bread and put it in the breadbox where it is objectively present despite my belief to the contrary. Likewise, I can even have bread objectively present in my mouth without believing it: suppose for instance I inattentively pop a piece of bread in my mouth thinking it is a bit of rice cake. The bread is present in my mouth even though I don't believe it. In precisely this sense, according to both Lutheran and Roman Catholic views, Christ's body is objectively present in the mouth of all who partake in the sacrament, whether they believe it or not.[321]

If the body and blood of Christ are objectively present in the eating of the bread and drinking of the cup, then by necessity, it follows that both are received by all who partake. For those who reject this reality, Paul's warning seems spurious at best. If all they are eating and drinking is bread and wine, how can those who eat in an unworthy manner "eat" and "drink" judgment unto themselves apart from Christ's true presence?

The Bread We Break for a Broken Body

1 Corinthians 10:17

Because there is one bread, we who are many are one body, for we all partake of the one bread.

The New Testament meal established by Jesus was not intended for the twelve alone, but for his body the church to show forth his death until he returns.[322] What Jesus instituted in the upper room was not

---

[321]Cary, "The Eucharistic Presence in Calvin," lines 13–20.

[322]Paul's discussion throughout 1 Cor 10–12 involves a play on the Greek word "body" (*soma*) as he uses it interchangeably to refer to Christ's bread/body in the Lord's Supper and to his body, the Church.

a sacrifice, but a sacrament, whereby those who ate and drank were made beneficiaries of the sacrifice that would take place the very next day. For Luther the primary and overarching gift of the Supper is the forgiveness of sins. For there we meet the Lamb of God, who takes away the sin of the world. Luther refused to compromise that in the Supper we really receive what the words declare. Forde notes its significance for Luther:

> Again the point is that God really comes down to earth to us; we do not ascend to him in heaven. The kind of forgiveness one gets from God is not a mere announcement from heaven or a lecture about forgiveness which we then have to work up the ability to believe, but a forgiveness which is actually *worked* in us by the very descent of God into things humble and lowly, into earthen vessels. That is why he made the "is" in "This *is* my body," "This *is* my blood," into a virtual watchword of the Lutheran Reformation.[323]

It is unfortunate that there has been so much confusion and conflict surrounding a sacrament that brings, as one of its corollary benefits, unity to the body of Christ. Thus we pray, "Come, Lord Jesus!"

---

[323]Forde, *Where God Meets Man*, 80.

ROUND 7

Kept in the True Faith

Apostasy and Assurance

A popular method of presenting the major tenets of Reformed theology has been through the "Five Points of Calvinism" developed at
the Synod of Dort (1618–1619) in response to the rise of Arminian-
ism. "Though it is a mistake to reduce the beliefs of Calvinism to five
emphases," cautions Horton, "it is true that most of the objections
and attacks on Calvinism focus on certain doctrinal distinctives."[324]
Those familiar with these five doctrinal distinctives likely learned
them from the acronym TULIP: (1) Total depravity, (2) Uncondi-
tional election, (3) Limited atonement, (4), Irresistible grace, and
(5) Perseverance of the saints.

In this concluding chapter, I will present some objections to
the "P" of the TULIP as I contrast it with a Lutheran understanding
of being kept in the faith. It will become necessary, in so doing, to
return and build upon several related doctrines discussed in earlier
chapters.

Perseverance of the Saints

The Westminster Confession states, "They whom God has accepted
in His Beloved, effectually called and sanctified by His Spirit, can
neither totally nor finally fall away from the state of grace: but shall

---

[324]Horton, *For Calvinism*, 15.

certainly persevere therein to the end, and eternally be saved."[325] The Reformed doctrine of the "perseverance of the saints" teaches that any person who has been regenerated by the Holy Spirit and justified by faith will remain in such a state to the end, because falling away from the faith is ruled an impossibility for a genuine believer. Sproul adds:

> A simple way to remember the essence of the doctrine of perseverance is to learn this ditty: "If we have it, we never lose it. If we lose it, we never had it." This is a cute way of affirming that full and final apostasy is never the lot of the Christian. Another short-hand expression of this doctrine is the aphorism, "Once saved, always saved." This is sometimes called eternal security, since it calls attention to the enduring power of the salvation wrought for us and in us by the work of Christ.[326]

Lutherans, by contrast, contend the Bible does not teach a "once saved, always saved" doctrine of perseverance, because there are numerous passages that clearly demonstrate that some people do experience true conversion for a time and then fall from grace by rejecting Christ and running their faith aground (1 Tim 1:19–20). Before we investigate a few of these passages, let me first positively state what Lutherans do teach concerning perseverance, as we are in agreement with the Reformed on some important points.

Preservation of the Elect

Romans 8:29–30

For those whom he foreknew he also predestined to be conformed to the image of his Son, that his Son would be the firstborn among many brothers and sisters. [30]And those he predestined, he also called; and those he called, he also justified; and those he justified, he also glorified.

---

[325]Westminster Confession, XVII, 1.

[326]Sproul, *What is Reformed Theology*, 197–198.

I begin the Lutheran doctrine of perseverance with an acknowledgement that all those chosen in Christ before the foundation of the world according to God's good pleasure will be brought to faith in the manner, and through the means, appointed by himself, and shall be saved (Eph 1:3–13). Paul comforted the Romans with this reality as he tells them they are predestined, called, justified, and glorified. Together this soteriological chain constitutes God's eternal plan to redeem the world. Absolutely nothing will separate the elect from the love of God in Christ (Rom 8:39).

Paul extols God as the primary actor in this redemptive drama. Each link in the chain is written in the past tense, which surprisingly includes, "glorified." Glorification is both a present possession (now) and a future promise (not yet), because of God's eternal purpose. Thus, Jesus could say of his elect flock, "I give them eternal life, and they will never perish; no one will snatch them from my hand" (John 10:28). Paul confidently affirmed the same, "For I am sure of this very thing, that the one who began a good work in you will perfect it until the day of Christ Jesus" (Phil 1:6). Nygren notes the objective nature of God's eternal plan:

> These are mighty affirmations which are closely knit together and stretch *from eternity—through time—to eternity*. The concept of the two aeons is here transcended. Before the old aeon stands God's eternal purpose. "Before the foundation of the world" God fixed his purpose of election. It is that which now moves on toward realization in the world, when God calls and justifies men. And it is that which He will bring to consummation in eternity, when He glorifies them. Paul would thus show how everything—from the eternal election to the final glory—is utterly in God's hand. There is place for neither chance nor arbitrariness.[327]

What God purposed to do in eternity he unfailingly carries out in time. The doctrine of election, furthermore, is always Christocentric in Scripture. Jesus Christ is *the* Elect One. Those whom Paul says God "foreknew" or "marked out beforehand" to be conformed to

---

[327]Nygren, *Romans*, 340.

the image of his Son are what they are because they are *in Christ*, the eternally known, chosen, elect Son and Savior.[328]

Thus far the Reformed would assent; however, the preservation of the elect does not negate the following truths of equal importance that stand alongside the passages that speak of election:

1. Universal Grace: God truly desires the salvation of all people (1 Tim 2:4);
2. Universal Atonement: Jesus died for the sins of the entire world (2 Cor 5:19);
3. Apostasy: There are genuine believers who reject Christ and fall from grace (Gal 5:4).

The first two points were sufficiently covered in chapter one, leaving us with the third point concerning apostasy. As we consider the biblical texts that follow, it will become clear that Lutherans accept the tensions presented in the New Testament concerning predestination, conversion, and apostasy. As I've mentioned throughout this book, Lutherans will go as far as the Bible leads, but never beyond. We confess that some truths remain a mystery only to be resolved in the age to come. David Scaer notes that our willingness to live with this tension is a distinctive mark of our theology:

> This tension between universal atonement and the reality that there are many who are eternally lost has been called the *crux theologorum*, a cross which the theologian must carry. Each attempt to reconcile rationally the unlimited atonement and the limited election leads to a denial of one or the other. The Holy Scriptures do not permit us to teach that Christ died for the elect only and that the lost were not included in the gracious will of God for all men. The same Scripture also does not permit us to teach that man can contribute anything to his salvation. Election was made in the eternal counsels of God and is not dependent on human choice or confirmation, even though election always results in a willing and in a certain sense, free choice. Conversion follows election and is totally dependent on it. Thus the

---

[328]See Calvin, *Institutes*, 3.24.5, where he also stresses this point.

distinctive mark of Lutheran theology is that it holds to a universal atonement and limited election.[329]

Apostasy: Hypothetical, Impossible, or Real Possibility?

Calvinists believe that God's grace is irresistible, so that once a person is converted and justified, he can never truly fall from grace. The Canons of Dort admit that believers may fall into gross sin, incur guilt, grieve the Holy Spirit, interrupt the exercise of faith, wound their consciences, and for a time lose the sense of God's favor, but God will never wholly withdraw the Holy Spirit even in their grievous falls; nor does he allow them to proceed so far as to lose the grace of adoption and forfeit the state of justification.[330] This stance, held also by the early Anabaptists, is rejected in Article XII of the Augsburg Confession on the basis of biblical passages that warn Christians against falling away, as well as those that provide examples of actual apostates.

The Warning Passages of Hebrews

The Bible is replete with passages that warn its listeners of the dire consequences of turning away from the salvation God has provided through Jesus Christ. Presbyterian theologian, Robert Peterson, numbers forty-four in the New Testament alone, chief among these are the five presented in the letter to the Hebrews.[331]

Hebrews lacks the traditional epistolary opening, so the author and his audience remain anonymous. The body of the letter, however, clearly addresses a specific group of Christians with intimate knowledge of their spiritual context and condition. The writer delineates his work as a "word of exhortation" (13:22), leading many to conclude that it was originally a sermon delivered to communities of Jewish Christians who were tempted to revert back to Judaism due to social pressures and the rise of persecution. The chief purpose of the letter,

---

[329]Scaer, "Nature and Extent of the Atonement," 180.

[330]Canons of Dort, Fifth Head, Articles 5 and 6.

[331]Peterson, "Apostasy in the Hebrews Warning Passages," 27, where he lists Heb 2:1–4; 3:7–4:13; 5:11–6:12; 10:19–39; and 12:1–29.

therefore, is to stop the spiritual regression of this church by exhorting them toward maturation and perseverance in the faith. The concern is not sin in general, but with the sin of unbelief. In addition to the warnings, the author also offers pastoral encouragement by saying he is convinced of better things concerning their salvation (6:9).

There is no Calvinist consensus on how to interpret the warning passages, and to interact with each and every writer would take us beyond the scope of this chapter. Nevertheless, what all Calvinist interpretations hold in common is that they go to great exegetical lengths to protect their doctrine of perseverance. Broadly speaking, Reformed apologists fall into one of two views.

The Hypothetical View. This view contends that the warnings are real, but the sin of apostasy has neither been committed nor can it be committed since true believers cannot fall away.[332] Sproul holds a nuanced version of this view. The passages address real believers, according to Sproul, but the warnings are simply a *reductio ad absurdum* argument making use of a hypothetical sin the writer knew his audience would never commit, since the author to Hebrews nowhere states that a true believer does in fact do what he is warning believers not to do.[333]

The False Believer View. Proponents of this view contend that the warnings are real and directed toward those in the congregation who truly can commit the sin, but those who can commit this sin are not genuine believers. It is argued that in every congregation there are unbelievers (tares) worshiping amongst true believers (wheat). They may look and sound like the real deal, sharing a common religious experience to include Baptism and the Lord's Supper, but the very fact that the sin of apostasy is a possibility for them proves their faith is fraudulent. As an advocate of the classical Reformed view, Buist Fanning says the author portrays these readers in distinctly Christian terms to emphasize how close they have been to the faith and what they are rejecting if they depart.[334]

---

[332]McKnight, "The Warning Passages of Hebrews," 23.

[333]Sproul, *What is Reformed Theology?*, 213–216.

[334]Fanning, "Classical Reformed View," *Four Views*, 217, sometimes called the "phenomenological-false believer view."

Contrary to both views, Lutherans affirm the warnings contained in Hebrews presuppose the possibility that true Christians can commit apostasy. Furthermore, as I will argue, the description in 6:4–6 makes it abundantly clear that the readers were considered by the author to be genuine Christians, not just in outward appearance.

The Danger of Apostasy

Hebrews 6:4–6

For it is impossible in the case of those who have once been enlightened, tasted the heavenly gift, become partakers of the Holy Spirit, ⁵tasted the good word of God and the miracles of the coming age, ⁶and then have committed apostasy, to renew them again to repentance, since they are crucifying the Son of God for themselves all over again and holding him up to contempt.

We will limit ourselves to two questions in examining this passage: (1) Who is the audience in danger of committing this sin? (2) Why is committing this sin so dangerous?

The Audience in Danger

Scot McKnight is correct that no issue is more crucial to the exegesis of Hebrews and its impact on soteriology than a clear determination of the audience to whom the author writes.[335] The author describes those tempted to "fall away" with four participles, each of these governed by the single article *tous* (those who), indicating a single group of people is in view. They are described in the following manner.

Once enlightened (6:4a).

The word "enlightened" is a common term in both the Old and New Testaments to designate the act of God by which he enlightens humanity with the revelation of his redemption.[336] The other use of "enlightened" in Hebrews is found in 10:32, where the writer reminds his readers of the harsh sufferings they endured following their "enlightenment" to Christ. Here the word is used as a synonym

---

[335]McKnight, "The Warning Passages of Hebrews," 43.

[336]See Isa 60:1, 19; Mic 7:8; 1 Cor 4:5; Eph 1:18, 3:9, 5:14; 2 Tim 1:10.

for conversion. Paul said the Ephesians had the eyes of their hearts "enlightened," so that they would know the hope to which they had been called (Eph 1:18).

To be "enlightened" was frequently connected to Baptism in the early church, but as many commentators point out, there is no certainty that a baptismal reference is being made here. Nevertheless, enlightenment is one of the effects of baptism as we learned in chapter four.

A basic grasp of the grammar the author employs enriches our understanding of the author's intent:

> The use of the aorist in this and the following three participles is significant. It seems to imply a certain definite finality in the events described. Also note the passive voice. This "enlightenment," whether it be conversion or baptism, is *God's* act. It is in God's light, not his own, that man sees light (Ps 36:9). There is no self-achievement here, no finding of knowledge by human power or pursuit. He who is "enlightened" is found by the Truth, and, therefore, should regard himself as one of the privileged poor, the illiterate bankrupt whom the Father has chosen to illumine (Matt 11:27).[337]

Tasted the heavenly gift (6:4b).

The term "taste" is used throughout the Bible in both a literal and figurative sense. Here it is employed as an idiom for experiencing the reality of the gift of heaven (cf. 1 Pet 2:3). To the sense of sight the writer adds taste in order to describe the inner, personal experience of salvation.[338]

Some Calvinists attempt a way around this by making a sharp distinction between "tasting" (partial participation) and "eating" (full participation). Roger Nicole asserts this group of people may have nibbled at the Christian faith, but in no way did they fully digest it.[339] However, this interpretation runs contrary to how "taste" is used elsewhere in the letter. For example, Hebrews 2:9 says Jesus "tasted" death for everyone. Surely Calvinists would not suggest that Jesus merely toyed with death in a partial manner?

---

[337]Hohenstein, "A Study of Hebrews 6:4–8," 438.

[338]Lenski, *Hebrews*, 182.

[339]Nicole, "Some Comments on Hebrews 6:4–6," 360–361.

But what of the phrase "heavenly gift?" Following Spiq, the term "gift" can be understood in a technical sense equal to grace.[340] As the taste of death in 2:9 means to experience the sorrow of death in all its fullness, so to taste the heavenly gift means to experience the full joy of receiving the gift of grace that can only come from heaven. Thus the phrase has often been linked with the Lord's Supper, the heavenly meal where we receive Christ's presence and pardon. The adjective "heavenly" thus denotes the source and location from which this gift is dispensed for us to taste here on earth. Hohenstein captures the Trinitarian nature of this gift:

> The whole New Testament consistently asserts that it is the Spirit who gifts life. Syllogistically speaking, we could say, "Apart from the Spirit no man can confess Jesus as Lord (1 Cor 12:3). Therefore, apart from the Spirit there is no life, for Jesus is *the* life." That makes the gift of heavenly life and the Spirit inseparable. The gift is life, the Giver is the Spirit, and, in a sense, the "Father of lights, from whom comes down every good and perfect gift" (Jas 1:17). Thus, to "taste the heavenly gift" involves a deeply absorbing experience with the Trinity itself. The "heavenly gift" is God Himself in the person of Christ descending upon His sin-ruined creation to effect its recreation. And it is all a *gift*, "not of works, lest any man should boast" (Eph 2:8, where God's gift equals salvation).[341]

Partakers of the Holy Spirit (6:4c).
The word "partake" (*metoxos*) is employed several times in the letter to denote companionship, participation, or sharing in common. He refers to his readers as "holy brothers, partners (*metoxoi*) in a heavenly calling" (Heb 3:1). These holy brothers and sisters were "enlightened" and "tasted the heavenly gift," because they had truly participated in the ministry of the Holy Spirit—the Lord and giver of life. Nicole concedes the word *metoxoi* here "appears to lend support to the view that true Christians are described here."[342]

---

[340]Spiq, *L'Epitre aux Hebreux*, 2:150–151.

[341]Hohenstein, "A Study of Hebrews 6:4–8," 439.

[342]Nicole, "Some Comments on Hebrews 6:4–6," 360.

Tasted the good word of God and the power of the age to come (6:5)
The Greek term used here for "word" is *rhema*, a reference to the utterances or teachings of God. One of the things that makes this deliberate sin so egregious is that they had received "knowledge of the truth" (10:26). Since this congregation had "participated in the Holy Spirit," it is only natural that they had also "tasted the good word of God," as Jesus had promised the disciples he would send the Spirit to guide them into all truth (John 16:13–15).

They had also experienced the "power of the age to come," which is a sign of the writer's inaugurated eschatology. For those unfamiliar with this concept, Berkhof summarizes, "In short, in the New Testament the future is the unfolding and completion of that which already exists in Christ and the Spirit and which will be carried through triumphantly in spite of sin, suffering, and death."[343] Throughout the Bible, the Holy Spirit is understood preeminently as the eschatological gift, the revealer of the new age. In Paul's letters especially, the reception of the Spirit means that one has become a participant in a new realm of existence associated with the future age, and now partakes in the "powers of the age to come."[344] The present gift of the indwelling Spirit is but a down payment of the full inheritance that is to come (Eph 1:14).

How do Reformed theologians deal with these descriptions? Those who advance the *false believer* view, answer:

> Those who apostatize have been beneficiaries of the Spirit's ministry through the means of grace even as merely formal or external members of the covenant community. Having been baptized ("enlightened"), they have also "*tasted* the heavenly gift" in the Supper and "*tasted* the goodness of the word of God and the powers of the age to come," but they have not actually received or *fed upon* Christ for eternal life, which Jesus linked to faith (Jn 6:27–58, 62–65).[345]

---

[343]Berkhof, *Well-Founded Hope*, 19.

[344]For the development of this theme in the Bible, see Hoekema, *Bible and the Future*, chs. 1 and 2.

[345]Horton, *Christian Faith*, 683, emphasis original, which highlights that *tasted* equates with a partial experience in Horton's estimation.

The descriptions, according to Horton, speak of the phenom-
enological experiences of the means of grace in the local church,
such as receiving catechesis, Baptism, and the Lord's Supper, but in
no way denote the spiritual reality. Again we find the sacraments
in the Reformed tradition amount to little more than symbolic signs
that advertise God's grace, but do not confer it, since these members were never saved. Fanning remarks, "Up to that point they had
given every evidence of true Christian experience."[346] Perhaps they
had given every evidence of a true Christian experience because
they were, from the author's own pastoral experience, true Christians? Absolutely nothing in the letter suggests otherwise.

Together these four phrases describe a rich and genuine Christian experience. If they are not enough evidence to prove the author
understood his audience to be genuinely converted, I would add the
following four points.

First, the writer addresses his audience as *brothers* (3:1; 10:19;
13:22), *beloved* (6:9), *believers* (4:3), *holy* (3:1), *sharers in a heavenly
calling* (3:1), and *sanctified by Christ's blood* (10:29).

Second, they are exhorted to move on to Christian maturity in
5:11–6:3, which assumes they had already experienced the beginning of their Christian walk. The issue was not the absence of faith,
but their immaturity in the faith.

Third, the writer says it is impossible for those who fall away
to *renew them again to repentance* (6:6). Sproul admits this phrase
presupposes they have repented at least once in the past. He adds,
"If repentance is, as Reformed theology believes, a fruit of regeneration, then the author of Hebrews is describing people who have been
regenerated."[347]

Fourth, if the recipients of these warnings are not believers, the
warnings seem strangely worded. Rather than a warning against falling away from a faith they do not actually possess, I would expect
evangelistic exhortations to repent and believe.

---

[346]Fanning, "Classical Reformed View," *Four Views*, 216.

[347]Sproul, *What is Reformed Theology?*, 214.

The Danger of the Sin

There is considerable consensus among commentators regarding the nature of the sin being warned against. The participle *parapesontas* (fall away) is ambiguous and best interpreted in light of its immediate context and from synonyms used throughout the letter.[348] The participles in Heb 6:6 should be translated in a temporal sense, that is to say, it is impossible to renew an apostate to repentance "as long as," or "while," they are rejecting Christ.[349] Renewal is possible for those who seek the Lord in repentance and faith (e.g. David and Peter), but it is impossible for one who rejects (and continues to reject) the Lord. As such, the sin of apostasy is distinct from the ongoing struggle with sin that befalls all believers. As Hagner writes:

> These Jewish Christian readers, who had so clearly participated in the fruit of Christian salvation, now contemplated turning away from it all. Nothing could be more serious in our author's view. He insists that their apostasy would be a form of betrayal and the shocking equivalent of crucifying Jesus and subjecting him to public shame yet once again. In effect, their apostasy would be a mockery of the cross itself.[350]

This reason apostasy is so dangerous is because of its severe consequences: *there is no way of escape* (2:2); *not entering Christ's*

---

[348]The author employs a variety of expressions for this sin: *slip away* (2:1); *disobedience* (2:2); *harden your hearts* (3:8, 13, 15; 4:7); *rebellion* (3:8, 15); *wander* (3:10); *unbelieving heart* (3:12); *apostasy* (3:12); *fall* (4:11); *fall away* (6:6); *giving up meeting together* (10:25); *deliberately sinning* (10:26); *contempt for the Son of God and insulting the Spirit of Grace* (10:29); *shrink back* (10:39); *sin that so easily entangles* (12:1); *grow weary and give up* (12:3); *forgotten the word of exhortation* (12:5); *coming short of the grace of God* (12:15); and to *reject the one who warns from heaven* (12:25).

[349]It states a time frame in which the action of the main verb is true, rather than seeing it in a causal sense. The modifying participles are *present* tense, not past. Since *present* participles typically refer to an action that is contemporaneous with the main verb, it makes for a more accurate translation to connect them to the main verb with words such as "while" or "as long as" (as the NASB and NET translator's notes allow).

[350]Hagner, *Encountering Hebrews*, 90.

rest (3:11–4:11); *impossible to renew unto repentance* (6:4–6); *no sacrifice for sins remains* (10:26); *judgment and fire* (10:27); *vengeance and retribution* (10:30–31); and *destruction* (10:39).[351] The rejection of Christ is tantamount to the burning of spiritual bridges, a fact that takes one to the point of no return. Apostasy therefore signals finality; it is called the "unforgivable sin" because it is the denial of the only One who is authorized to grant forgiveness. Those who worry about whether they have committed this sin demonstrate by such concern that they have not committed it.

Such warnings are not isolated to the book of Hebrews. In addressing the Judaizers in Galatia, Paul warned, "You who are trying to be declared righteous by the law have been alienated from Christ; you have fallen away from grace!" (Gal 5:4). Those who sought to be justified by the Law had rejected Christ, for Paul said they had deserted the one who called them by the grace and followed another gospel (Gal 1:6). The fellowship they once enjoyed was now severed. By despising God's grace, they forfeited it.

To the Church at Corinth, Paul cautioned, "So let the one who thinks he is standing be careful that he does not fall" (1 Cor 10:12). In his follow-up letter, he adds, "Now because we are fellow workers, we also urge you not to receive the grace of God in vain" (2 Cor 6:1). The genuineness of their faith is not in doubt, for he calls them his coworkers in ministry. The force of his warning is that God's grace can be received in vain by falling away.

Paul exhorted Timothy to fight the good fight, "To do this you must hold firmly to faith and a good conscience, which some have rejected and so have suffered shipwreck in regard to the faith. Among these are Hymenaeus and Alexander, whom I handed over to Satan to be taught not to blaspheme" (1 Tim 1:19–20). We learn from his second letter that Hymenaeus had begun to teach false doctrine (2 Tim 2:17–18); and later, that Alexander did Paul a great deal of harm (2 Tim 4:14). What did they reject and shipwreck? Their "faith" and a "good conscience," demonstrating they once genuinely possessed them, for you cannot run a hypothetical ship aground.

---

[351]These are describing far more than just a loss of future eternal rewards as some commentators suggest.

When you tally the cumulative descriptions and examples of apostasy and its resultant consequences in the New Testament, it is hard to grasp how some Reformed interpreters can conclude the warning passages are hypothetical—a clever ruse to rouse believers to maturity. Sproul recognizes that the author is employing what Luther called the "evangelical use of the law" in the admonitions of Hebrews.[352] The law does reveal the greatness of our sin and our desperate need for God's grace and forgiveness. The problem with Sproul's view is the law has been reduced to a toothless rhetorical device, a spectacular warning against an imaginary disaster that will never occur. Proponents of this view, in my opinion, do not take the law seriously enough. It smacks of an artificiality unbecoming the holiness of God who is called a "consuming fire" (Heb 12:29).

Bishop Ryle once noted a concern I share, "I have long come to the conclusion that men may be more systematic in their statements than the Bible, and may be led into grave error by idolatrous veneration of a system."[353] In order to preserve a doctrine that fits the paradigm of their system, Calvinists are forced to make erroneous assumptions contrary to the plain sense of the warning passages. All who are concerned with biblical fidelity should heed Hagner's advice by listening to all that God's Word has to say on a given subject, even when it creates dissonance for our theological systems:

> We do well to limit ourselves to the full scope of the specific statements of Scripture, the raw data of biblical theology, and to preserve the tensions we encounter therein . . . It is not a question of refusing to think through these matters clearly and consistently, or of throwing logic to the winds, but rather, of listening to all that Scripture has to say on an issue. We must not let our theological system cancel out one side or the other of biblical teaching, even if presently the various materials appear to be incompatible.[354]

---

[352]Sproul, *What is Reformed Theology?*, 215, often called the 2nd use or function of the Law.

[353]Ryle, *Expository Thoughts on the Gospels*, 3:157.

[354]Hagner, *Encountering Hebrews*, 91.

God's Grace: Received and Resisted

Salvation is the gift of a gracious God for the sake of the complete and meritorious work of Jesus Christ (Eph 2:8–10). The faith that justifies is created in the heart of sinners solely and exclusively by the Holy Spirit, who is active through the means of grace.[355] Thus confessional Lutherans reject every form of synergism. Before conversion we are entirely incapable—in any way—of responding to or cooperating with God's grace.[356]

At the same time, we reject the Calvinist thesis that God does not desire to convert and save all humanity (particular grace). Many who hear the Good News indeed remain unconverted, but solely because they stubbornly resist the gracious operation of the Holy Spirit.

Holding these biblical truths in tension perplexes Reformed theologians, because on the one hand, we strongly affirm a monergistic soteriology (God alone saves); while on the other hand, we contend with equal vigor to a universal atonement and the possibility of resisting the Spirit's inward calling through the outward gospel. For Horton, this represents an *inconsistent monergism*. He asks, "How can one say that God alone saves, from beginning to end, while also affirming the possibility of losing one's salvation?"[357]

First, although God is the sole author of saving faith, we retain our character as personal beings in conversion. Though we were dead in our trespasses and sins (Eph 2:1), God did not make us alive through the gospel as though we were automatons made of wood or metal. Divine monergism, in other words, does not mean that God coerces us with an irresistible force; but rather, the Spirit recreates and influences us as his children in a manner that comports with our personality as humans born "from above" according to God's gracious will (John 1:12–13).

Second, while we do not cooperate in our conversion, once we are converted, we do work with the Spirit to sustain our faith through the same means he used to call and convert us, namely, through the

---

[355] Augsburg Confession V, *Triglotta*, 45.

[356] Formula of Concord, Epitome II, *Concordia*, 495.

[357] Horton, *Christian Faith*, 686.

Word and Sacraments.[358] Mueller notes that any activity which seems to be cooperation or a participatory action by humans is actually a consequence of conversion and thus is more accurately understood and explained as part of our sanctification.[359] Horton affirms the same when he says that sanctification includes our own activity as enabled by God's grace.

> We were not active but acted upon by the Spirit through the gospel. However, as those who are now alive in Christ, we are exhorted, "[W]ork out your own salvation with fear and trembling; for it is God who works in you, both to will and to work for his good pleasure (Phil 2:12–13). Although we cannot work *for* our own salvation, we can and must work *out* that salvation in all areas of our daily practice, realizing more and more the amazing truth of our identity in Jesus Christ.[360]

How then can people resist and reject God's grace if God is the one doing all the saving? While it will not satisfy the consistency Calvinism demands, Luther's axiom remains the most consistent answer the Bible will grant: When God works through *means*, he can be resisted; when God operates *without means*, in his uncovered majesty, he cannot be resisted. Pieper explains:

> When God deals with us through his Word and says, "Come unto me . . ." (Matt 11:28), resistance is possible; so Christ reports: "Ye would not" (Matt 23:37). But when Christ will appear on Judgment Day in His uncovered majesty ("in His glory"), all resistance is excluded, for "before Him shall be gathered all nations," etc. (Matt 26:31–32). The statement, therefore, of the supporters of a *gratia particularis* that when God earnestly desires a thing, no man can resist His will must be changed, on the basis of Scripture, to read that when God works through means, and earnestly means to accomplish His

---

[358]"After conversion and because of Christ, the new man in us does in fact respond to and cooperate with God the Holy Spirit," Formula of Concord, Epitome II, *Concordia*, 495.

[359]Mueller, *Called to Believe, Teach, and Confess*, 269.

[360]Horton, *Christian Faith*, 662.

purpose, His will can be resisted. Thus the whole Calvinistic argument that the "result" is the correct interpretation of the will of God falls to the ground.[361]

Contrary to the "I" in the Calvinist TULIP (irresistible grace), Lutherans contend that one of the great mysteries of the faith is that God's grace is resistible, because God does not come to us in unveiled majesty (naked), but accommodates himself to our human condition by using the tangible means of grace (clothed) to convert sinners. Let us consider two examples.

Matthew 23:37 (ESV)

O Jerusalem, Jerusalem, the city that kills the prophets and stones those who are sent to it! How often would I have gathered your children together as a hen gathers her brood under her wings, and you would not.

Here amidst the crowds in Jerusalem, Jesus laments the rejection of his love. Just as a mother hen gathers her chicks under her outstretched wings to shield them from harm, so Jesus had longed to gather Jerusalem into his kingdom to save them from the judgment to come; but like unruly chicks, they obstinately resist his will. Here Jesus exposes two things pertinent to our discussion: (1) What he had often willed to do (*How often would I have . . .*); and (2) What Jerusalem, just as often, had resisted (*and you would not*).

Acts 7:51

You stubborn people, with uncircumcised hearts and ears! You are always resisting the Holy Spirit, like your ancestors did!

As Stephen sat before an obstinate Jewish council, he summarized all the promissory benefits that God had provided his covenant people. God had left nothing undone to save them, yet they had rejected Moses (7:35), persecuted and killed the prophets that foretold the

---

[361]Pieper, *Christian Dogmatics*, 2:30.

coming Messiah (7:52), and now they stood ready to repeat this long history of violence by killing another one of God's mouthpieces.

The verb for resistance in the Greek literally means to "fall against" (*antipipto*). By resisting the inspired word of the apostles, they were "falling against" the Holy Spirit, who is in and with the Word they preached. Irresistible grace for Calvinists means that the sinner's resistance to the grace of regeneration cannot thwart the Spirit's purpose.[362] But this is exactly what Stephen tells the stiff-necked council they were doing—just as their fathers had done.

Passages such as these are problematic for the Calvinist position as they demonstrate the will of God is resistible. To get around this, the Calvinist must go in one of two directions:

1. Those who resist the Holy Spirit can do so, they reason, because they are non-elect. What they are resisting is not "irresistible" (or effectual) grace, but merely "common" grace, since God is not sincerely concerned with saving them.[363]
2. God's will is divided into two distinct classes, such as "revealed" and "sovereign," so that when the scripture speaks of people resisting God's will, it is only his "revealed" will, not his "sovereign" will, which is what matters in salvation.[364]

The first option is untenable as Jesus clearly longs for more than Jerusalem's general well-being. His lamentation specifically addresses their rejection of his desire to gather them into his kingdom, where they would be saved from the judgment to come. For this was his purpose for being in Jerusalem (i.e. to go to the cross). Furthermore, Stephen was not murdered for offering a generic meditation on God's providential care, but because he boldly recited the long history of God's saving promises and deeds culminating in the betrayal and death of Jesus Christ (Acts 7:52). And since Calvinists cannot pretend to know the

---

[362]Sproul, *What is Reformed Theology*, 189.

[363]See pg. 5–6 for my critique of common grace.

[364]So Horton, *Christian Faith*, 263.

secret decrees of God any more than Lutherans, it seems presumptuous to declare who is elect and not, based upon the evidence of the text. We certainly would not want to rush to conclusions about Saul, the young man mentioned at the end of Acts 7:59 before getting to 9:15.

The second option dividing the will of God is systematic sleight-of-hand to divert our attention away from what the passages actually say. In an effort to defend God's sovereignty, Calvinists create an entirely new problem by making God's will(s) self-contradictory. Gerhard noted the trouble with this approach long ago, "Those who attribute contradictory wills to God weaken the simplicity of the divine essence, for where there are contradictions in the wills, there is no room for the highest and most perfect simplicity."[365]

We have already discussed how Luther spoke of God's hidden and revealed will, especially in relation to predestination, but this was not to divide the will of God; rather, it was to highlight the fact that the revealed will is the only one we have. God hides because he does not desire to be known in his naked majesty, but solely and exclusively in the Son he sent to redeem the world, as the Word testifies.

> God must therefore be left to himself in his own majesty, for in this regard we have nothing to do with him, nor has he willed that we should have anything to do with him. But we have something to do with him insofar as he is clothed and set forth in his word.[366]

Since we have something to do with God only in so far as he has, in merciful condescension to our limited comprehension, revealed and offered himself to us in Holy Scripture, we are on safe ground when we stick to the logic of Scripture, following the sequence of John 3:17–18:

---

[365]Gerhard, *Loci Theologici*, 1§131. As Lutherans were drawn into debates with Calvinists over predestination, our dogmaticians also attempted to classify God's will in a variety of ways (first/second, antecedent/consequent, etc.) with mixed results. Such endeavors ultimately led, in my opinion, to further confusion, and in some cases, gross error. For a short history, see Preus, *Post-Reformation Lutheranism*, 2:96–100.

[366]Luther, *Bondage of the Will*, LW, 33:139.

For God did not send his Son into the world to condemn the world, but that the world should be saved through him. [18]The one who believes in him is not condemned. The one who does not believe has been condemned already, because he has not believed in the name of the one and only Son of God.

God would have all humanity to be saved in his Son and only condemns those who refuse to believe. Gerhard said this is like a physician who stands ready to give precious medicine to all those afflicted with a disease, but has to bury those who stubbornly refuse to take it.[367] This is why Lutherans refuse to answer the *crux theologorum*—why some and not others—with anything but Scripture.

Why are some saved? The answer is God alone. *He did not send his Son into the world to condemn the world, but that the world should be saved through him. The one who believes in him is not condemned.*

Why are some condemned? The fault lies with those who refuse to believe. *The one who does not believe has been condemned already, because he has not believed in the name of the one and only Son of God.*

Natural reason is put off by this scriptural paradox and looks to solve the riddle by seeking the solution exclusively in God or in humanity. Calvinists link the salvation of one and the damnation of another to the divine decree (double predestination). Synergists link the salvation of one and the damnation of another to the free agency of humanity (free will). Holy Scripture says that whoever is saved is saved by God's grace alone; whoever is lost is so solely by his or her own unbelief. Preus concludes, "It is the emphatic and consistent teaching of Lutheran theology that man has the frightening capacity to resist God's will . . . If this cannot be harmonized with the single and immutable nature of God's will, Lutheran theology can only let the matter rest and remain silent before this mystery."[368]

---

[367]Gerhard, *Loci Theologici*, 1§271.

[368]Preus, *Post-Reformation Lutheranism*, 2:99.

Anxiety and Assurance: Finding Grace in the Right Place

Doubt, uncertainty, and anxiety possess the potential to paralyze faith. "A spirituality that fails to address and deal with such themes," McGrath maintains, "has strictly limited value as a resource for the Christian church."[369] As previously noted, Lutherans and Calvinists both share the belief that those whom God has predestined in Christ will persevere to the end. One unfortunate but common response to the doctrine of predestination is anxiety, leading some to doubt or despair over their salvation. Luther referred to such angst as *anfechtung*, an assault of the devil whose aim is to undermine faith in Christ. If only the elect persevere in faith, "How do I know if I am among the elect," asks the weary soul? Such concerns are where the rubber of perseverance meets the road of assurance.

Because of the doctrinal differences I've highlighted above, Calvinists and Lutherans possess their own unique set of pastoral problems associated with the assurance of salvation. If Christ died only for the elect, as Calvinists confess, they must confront the corollary concern of whether or not Christ died specifically for them, thus heightening the question of predestination. Likewise, if losing our salvation is a possibility for Christians, as Lutherans maintain, we must attend the associated anxiety of whether or not our faith will persevere. While the concerns may differ, assurance ultimately rests in the object of justifying faith.

"The person who does not have faith is like someone who has to cross the sea but is so frightened that he does not trust the ship. And so he stays where he is and is never saved, because he will not get on board and cross over."[370] Luther often made use of the Latin term *fiducia* for faith, which translates as "confidence" or "trust." A faith which justifies is not merely the belief that something is true; it is placing your confidence in the reliability of the one that justifies sinners. To use Luther's nautical analogy, faith is not simply believing a ship exists; it is about stepping into it and entrusting ourselves to it.[371] Moreover, confidence is not to be placed in the strength or

---

[369]McGrath, *Spirituality in an Age of Change*, 95.

[370]Cited by McGrath, *Reformation Thought*, 98.

[371]McGrath, *Reformation Thought*, 98.

intensity of our faith, and certainly not in our emotions, but in the treasure of Christ alone.

> Even if my faith is weak, I still have exactly the same treasure and the same Christ as others. There is no difference . . . It is like two people, each of whom owns a hundred guldens. One may carry them around in a paper sack, the other in an iron chest. But despite these differences, they both own the same treasure. Thus the Christ whom you and I own is one and the same, irrespective of the strength or weakness of your faith or mine.[372]

Faith justifies, not because of what faith is, but of what it apprehends. As the hand that receives a free gift does not merit the treasure, so faith cannot merit salvation, but only accepts it. Those who trust in their faith or depend upon the fruit of faith (good works) for reassurance, make a Christ out of their faith, and will never find the certainty their souls long for. The *subjective* state of the believer requires for its existence an unshakeable *objective* foundation.[373]

It is here that Calvinists depart from Lutherans in practice, which Cary describes as narrow but deep, like a small crack that goes a long ways down.[374] On the question of whether or not we are elect, Calvin generally follows Luther's caution against inquiring into the hidden will of God, but adds, "we shall follow the best order, if, in seeking the certainty of our election, we cleave to those posterior signs which are sure attestations to it."[375] Gerstner takes it a step further when he says the answer can be found indirectly by looking at our hearts and lives. "If in your heart you love the Lord Jesus Christ, and in your life of obedience to His commandments you are demonstrating that you sincerely trust Him and love Him, then you have life [thus proving you are elect]."[376] This approach has had the tendency

---

[372]Cited by McGrath, *Reformation Thought*, 99.

[373]See Schaller, *Biblical Christology*, 281–86.

[374]Cary, "Why Luther is Not Quite Protestant," 447.

[375]Calvin, *Institutes*, 3.24.4.

[376]Gerstner, *Primitive Theology*, 172. The Westminster Confession XVIII, 1, does state that "infallible assurance" does not belong to the essence of faith, meaning that assurance is not a necessary condition for salvation.

of making the "experience" of faith part and parcel with the "content" of faith, which robs the believer of the comfort for which they long. The justified sinner runs forever on a treadmill of uncertainty because his sin unavoidably fouls his best efforts to find proof of his election through good works. The anxiety that follows is amplified by the fact that many unbelievers refrain from evil and outwardly do good and charitable works that supersede those of believers.

When people came to Luther fretting over predestination, he cautioned them against pointless speculation, likening it to a fire that cannot be extinguished. Since there is no comfort to be found in the hidden God, Luther drew their attention again and again to the revealed God:

> [F]or this is how He set forth his will and counsel: "I will reveal My foreknowledge and predestination to you in an extraordinary manner, but not by this way of reason and carnal wisdom, as you imagine. This is how I will do so: From an unrevealed God I will become a revealed God. Nevertheless, I will remain the same God. I will be made flesh, or send my Son. He shall die for your sins and shall rise again from the dead. And in this way I will fulfill your desire, in order that you may be able to know whether you are predestined or not. Behold, this is My Son; listen to him (cf. Matt 17:5). Look at Him as He lies in the manger and on the lap of His mother, as he hangs on the cross. Observe what He does and what He says. There you will surely take hold of Me.[377]

While doubt and uncertainty plague all believers in some measure, they do not belong to the nature of saving faith, but the nature of unbelief. In this life, therefore, we will always need to echo the prayer, "Lord, I believe; help my unbelief" (Mark 9:24)! Luther reiterates this in his description of the daily life of the baptized: "Thus a Christian life is nothing else than a daily baptism, begun once and continuing ever after. For we must keep at it without ceasing, always purging whatever pertains to the old Adam, so that whatever belongs the new creature may come forth."[378] In other words, a Christian never outgrows the

---

[377]Luther, "Lectures on Genesis 26–30," LW, 5:42.

[378]Large Catechism, IV, 65, *Book of Concord*, 465.

need for justification—he remains a sinner although righteousness is imputed to him as he lives by faith. Since we are simultaneously saint and sinner, living by faith is a continuous necessity, not a once-for-all event. Sin remains, therefore, the need for repentance also remains. The life of faith is not a complacent reflection on past victories but an armed struggle.[379]

To arm believers and counteract temptation, anxiety, and doubt even in the face of death, God implemented Baptism, the Word, and the Supper. In a tender letter to his ailing mother, Luther provides us with an excellent example of evangelical pastoral care:

> You know the real basis and foundation of your salvation, on which you must rest your confidence in this and all troubles, namely, Jesus Christ, the cornerstone, who will never waver or fail us, nor allow us to sink and perish, for he is the Savior and he is called the Savior of all poor sinners, of all who face tribulation and death, of all who rely on him and call on his name . . . To such knowledge, I say, God has graciously called you. In the gospel, in Baptism, and the Sacrament (of the Altar) you possess his sign and seal of this vocation, and as long as your hear him addressing you in these, you will have no trouble or danger. Be of good cheer, then, and thank him joyfully for such great grace, for he who has begun a good work in you will perform until the day of Jesus Christ.[380]

If we turn once more to the exhortations in Hebrews we find similar counsel offered.

Hebrews 10:22–25 (ESV)

Let us draw near with a true heart in full assurance of faith, with our hearts sprinkled clean from an evil conscience and our bodies washed

---

[379]Trigg, *Baptism in the Theology of Luther*, 170. Cary makes an important distinction regarding the Reformed doctrine of perseverance, which effects all later Protestant thought on justification, generating a distinctively Protestant focus on conversion. "This explains why Protestants treat justification as happening only once in a lifetime, when we are converted to faith: For after that point, we are sure to be saved eternally," *History of Christian Theology*, 74.

[380]Tappert, *Luther's Letters*, 34–36; Luther's mother died a month later.

clean with pure water. ²³*Let us hold fast the confession of our hope without wavering, for he who promised is faithful.* ²⁴*And let us consider how to stir up one another to love and good works,* ²⁵*not neglecting to meet together, as is the habit of some, but encouraging one another, and all the more as you see the Day drawing near.*

The author provides a twofold strategy for being kept in true faith: trusting in the promises of grace and turning to the means of grace.

Trusting in the Promises of Grace

What motivation do we have to hold fast to the confession of our hope in the midst of trial and temptation? The promise of Christ! He remains faithful, even when we are not. The only foundation we have for assurance is the fact that God *tells* us that he laid down a foundation for us in Christ. It is a fact to be believed because he says so. This confidence is reflected in the *extra nos* emphasis of Luther's lectures on Galatians:

> And this is why our theology is certain; it snatches us away from ourselves and places us outside ourselves so that we do not depend on our own strength, conscience, experience, person or works, but depend on that which is outside ourselves, that is, on the promise and truth of God, which cannot deceive. [381]

We can "draw near with full assurance" because our faith is rigorously objective rather than subjective, since it is based upon Christ's shed blood and trustworthy promise. What makes faith certain is not the activity of the subject of faith (i.e. our strength, conscience, experience, person or works), but the faithfulness of the object of faith (he who promised is faithful). The Holy Spirit not only calls us to faith by the word of promise, but he continues to help us "hold fast to our confession of hope" by the same word of promise.

Turning to the Means of Grace

Where do we hear and experience this encouraging promise of grace? In the liturgy of the church, the place where Christians gather

---

[381]Luther, "Lectures on Galatians 1–4," LW, 26:387.

around God's Word and Sacraments. This is why the author to the Hebrews pleads with his audience to "not neglect meeting together." He reminds them of their identity as the baptized—their hearts *sprinkled* clean from an evil conscience and bodies *washed* with pure water (Heb 10:22). Baptism, Absolution, and the Lord's Supper not only confer justifying faith and the forgiveness of sins, but continue to sustain and strengthen the same in the ongoing battle against sin, the world, and the devil.

Wagner points out, "Vast multitudes in Christendom continue to neglect and despise God's Word and His Sacraments in spite of the fact that God Himself has ordained them and the Holy Spirit Himself has condescended to use them as a means of creating certainty in the heart."[382] The Lutheran tradition is unique among evangelicalism in recognizing the role of the sacramental Word in producing sanctification and the assurance of God's love and fidelity.

The mind reels and the heart soars when you stop to ponder the promise of the gospel. That God in infinite mercy should regard us treasonous rebels with such undeserving love to send his Son to atone for our sins, call and gift us with faith, declare us righteous in his sight, grant us the Holy Spirit, preserve us in faith, and, having predestined us, bring us to glory at long last, is a promise so incredible we begin to understand why King David wrote, "Your knowledge is beyond my comprehension; it is so far beyond me, I am unable to fathom it" (Ps 139:6). Heaven and earth will pass away, but Christ's word of promise remains; therefore, let us conclude with one of Luther's prayers:

> Eternal God and Father of our Lord Jesus Christ, grant us Your Holy Spirit who writes the preached word into our hearts so that we may receive and believe it, and be gladdened and comforted by it in eternity. Glorify Your Word in our hearts. Make it so bright and warm that we may find pleasure in it, and through Your inspiration think what is right. By Your power fulfill the Word, for the sake of Jesus Christ, Your Son, our Lord. Amen.

---

[382]Wagner, "Certainty of Salvation," *Abiding Word*, 1:227.

Post Script

A church historian, Douglas Sweeney, was asked on a popular Calvinist website if Luther was a Calvinist. The question may seem a bit naive now that you have read this book, but for many, Luther and his followers are known only through the filter of popular Reformed pastors and theologians. I am grateful that men like Sproul, Horton, and McGrath continue to find Luther's legacy important, even if they do not agree with all of his doctrinal positions. Sweeney's response underlines the unique place of Lutheran thought in the evangelical marketplace:

> The wrong thing to conclude from this evidence is that Lutherans are hesitant Calvinists, or two-and-a-half-point Calvinists, or imperfect Arminians. Lutherans are Lutherans. Their theological frame of reference is not closely related to the Calvinist–Arminian continuum. Lutherans have their own theological history, one that has contributed in major ways to the evangelical movement.[383]

Despite having a larger membership than the Reformed in North America, Lutherans, for a number of reasons, have never enjoyed the prominence or the influence of Calvinism. A historian once explained the reason for this was because Lutherans never learned to speak with an American accent, which is likely true. Lutherans are Lutheran. But we are also scripturally faithful, and this is why I am a Lutheran. As you wrestle with the biblical arguments that I have put forward, I pray you would be like the Bereans that Luke mentions in Acts 17:11. May you receive the message with great eagerness and examine the Scriptures to see if what I have said is true.

---

[383]Sweeney, "Was Luther a Calvinist," lines 375–385.

The Saxon Visitation Articles of 1592

A Contemporary Translation with Biblical Citations

Introduction

Following the death of Martin Luther in 1546, the Lutheran Church entered a tumultuous time over the next fifty years as an ecclesial game of back and forth was played in the German lands between Lutheranism, Roman Catholicism, and Calvinism according to the religious proclivities of political officer bearers. When Elector August of Saxony died in 1586, those surrounding his young son, Christian, included counselors and theologians who favored the theology of Geneva. Led by Christian's chancellor, Nikolaus Krell, he and other crypto-Calvinist leaders nullified the authority of the Book of Concord and replaced Lutheran professors and pastors with followers of Calvin.

After Christian's death five years later, his cousin Duke Wilhelm restored Lutheran theologians and pastors to key positions in the electoral Saxon court. To reestablish the Lutheran symbols and liturgical practices in local churches, Wilhelm commissioned the Visitation Articles of 1592, whose primary author was Aegidius Hunnius, a newly installed professor at Wittenberg. The articles were used to catechize churches in Lutheran doctrine through a series of pastoral visitations. Here the key differences between Calvinism and Lutheranism are brought into sharp focus in four succinctly written articles. They were appended to every edition of the Book of Concord published in Saxony until the forced union of Lutherans and Reformed under the Prussian Order of 1817.

I have taken liberty to rearrange the order of the articles by presenting the positive doctrinal statements of each article, followed by the corresponding negative statements rejecting the Calvinist position. Furthermore, I have translated them in a dynamic equivalent manner for ease in reading and understanding. Parenthetical Bible proofs are provided for support, but they were not included in the original text. Translation is based upon the German and Latin in Philip Schaff, *Bibliotheca Symbolica Ecclesia Universalis*, Vol. 3 (New York: Harper and Brothers, 1877), 181–89.

Article 1: The Lord's Supper

*The pure and true doctrine of our
church concerning the Holy Supper*

1. The words of Christ, "Take, eat, this is my body . . . drink, for this is my blood," are to be understood in their simple and literal sense, just as they read (Matt 26:26–28).
2. There are two things given and received in the sacrament: one earthy (bread and wine), and the other heavenly (body and blood; 1 Cor 10:16–17).
3. The giving and receiving of this sacramental union takes place on earth, and not in heaven (Acts 2:42).
4. The true and natural body of Christ that hung upon the cross and the true and natural blood that flowed from his side are given and received (1 Cor 11:23–26).
5. The body and blood of Christ are not only received spiritually by faith, which can take place apart from the Sacrament (cf. John 6:47–51), but they are also received by mouth together with the bread and wine, yet in a mysterious and supernatural manner, as a guarantee and assurance of the resurrection of our bodies from the dead (1 Cor 10:16–17).
6. The body and blood of Christ are received orally not only by the worthy, but also the unworthy, who partake without repentance and true faith. Both receive the body and blood of Christ with differing results: the worthy unto salvation; the unworthy unto judgment (1 Cor 11:27–34).

The false teaching of the Calvinists concerning the Lord's Supper

1. The words of institution are to be understood figuratively, and not as they plainly read.
2. There are only empty signs in the Supper as the body of Christ is as far away from the bread as the highest heaven is from the earth.
3. Christ is present in the Supper by his virtue and power, but not with his body, just as the splendor and presence of the sun is felt on earth, while existing far above the earth.
4. The body is only a type or figure of Christ's body, which is only signified and prefigured [by the bread].
5. The body is not received by the mouth, but through faith alone, raising us spiritually to heaven.
6. Only the worthy receive the body; the unworthy, who do not have faith to ascend into heaven, receive only bread and wine.

Article 2: The Person of Christ

*The pure and true doctrine of our
church concerning the person of Christ*

1. There are two distinct natures in Christ—divine and human. These remain for eternity and will never be confused or separated (John 1:1–14).
2. There is a personal union of these two natures, but only one person, Jesus Christ (1 Tim 2:4–5).
3. Because of this personal union, it is correct to say, since it is factually true, that God is man, and man is God; that Mary bore the Son of God (Gal 4:4), and that God redeemed us by his own true blood (Acts 20:28).
4. By this personal union and his subsequent exaltation, Christ has been seated at God's right hand according to his human nature and has received all power in heaven and on earth, and shares in all divine majesty, honor, power, and glory. (Matt 25:31, 28:19; Eph 4:8–10).

The false teaching of the Calvinists concerning the person of Christ

1. The expressions, "God is man" and "man is God," are understood as figurative speech.
2. The human nature has communion with the divine not in reality or truth, but only in name and words (i.e. anthropomorphic statements).
3. Despite his omnipotence, it is impossible for God to cause the natural body of Christ to be simultaneously present in more than one location.
4. By virtue of his exaltation and according to his human nature, Christ has received created gifts and finite power, but cannot know or do all things.
5. Christ rules in absentia according to his humanity, just as the King of Spain rules his new Islands from afar.
6. It is a damnable idolatry to place our trust and hope in Christ not only according to his divine nature, but also according to his human nature, and to honor and adore both natures.

Article 3: Holy Baptism

The pure and true doctrine of our church concerning Holy Baptism

1. There is only one Baptism and washing, not that which removes filth from the body, but one that cleanses us from our sins (1 Peter 3:21).
2. Baptism is a washing of regeneration and renewal in the Holy Spirit (Titus 3:5–7), whereby God saves us and works in us righteousness and cleansing from sin. The one who trusts and perseveres in this covenant to the end will not perish, but has eternal life (Col 2:11–13).
3. All who are baptized in Jesus Christ are baptized into his death, and therefore, buried with him in his death, having put on Christ through baptism (Rom 6:3–4; Gal 3:27).
4. Baptism is a washing of regeneration because in it we are born again and sealed by the Spirit of adoption through grace (Rom 8:15–17).

5. Unless a person is born again of water and the Spirit, he cannot enter the kingdom of heaven (John 3:5). This does not apply, however, to cases of necessity (e.g. emergencies where a person dies before they could be baptized).
6. That which is born of flesh is flesh (John 3:6); and by nature, we are all children of God's wrath, for we are born of sinful seed and conceived in sin (Ps 51:5; Rom 5:12; Eph 2:1–3).

The false teaching of the Calvinists concerning Holy Baptism

1. Baptism is an external washing of water by which an inner cleansing of sins is merely signified.
2. Baptism does not work nor confer regeneration, faith, the grace of God, and salvation, but only signifies and seals them.
3. Not all who are baptized with water receive the grace of Christ and the gift of faith, but the elect alone.
4. Regeneration does not occur in and with Baptism, but afterwards, in adulthood, and for some, not until old age.[384]
5. Since salvation does not depend on Baptism, emergency baptisms should not be permitted in the church. When a pastor of the church cannot be obtained, children should be allowed to die without Baptism.
6. The children of Christian parents are holy before Baptism in their mother's womb, and before birth are received into the covenant of eternal life; otherwise, the sacrament of Baptism could not be administered to them.

---

[384]Calvinists do not set age limitations on regeneration. This article likely reflects a distortion of Calvinist teaching prevalent at the time of writing. Nevertheless, Calvinists do link regeneration to the secret operation of the Holy Spirit through the means of the preached Word, and not to Baptism, as the article indicates.

Article 4: Predestination and the Eternal Providence of God

The pure and true doctrine of our church concerning on this article

1. Christ died for all humanity, and as the Lamb of God, he has taken away the sins of the whole world (John 1:29).
2. God created no one for condemnation, but desires that all to be saved and come to a knowledge of the truth (1 Tim 2:4). Therefore, he commands all to hear his Son Christ in the gospel and promises the power and efficacy of the Holy Spirit to convert and save those who hear the gospel (Rom 1:16–17).
3. Those condemned are so by their own guilt, unwilling to hear the gospel of Christ or by falling from grace; either through error against the foundation of our faith, or by sin against conscience (John 3:18; 1 Tim 1:19–20).
4. All sinners who repent are received into grace, and no one is excluded, even though their sins are as red as blood, for God's mercy is greater than the sin of the whole world, and God has compassion on all he has made (Ps 86:5).

The false teaching of the Calvinists concerning predestination and the providence of God

1. Christ did not die for all humanity, but only for the elect.
2. God created the greater part of humanity for eternal damnation and is unwilling that be converted and saved.
3. The elect and regenerate cannot lose faith and the Holy Spirit or be condemned, even though they commit great sins and every crime imaginable.
4. By necessity those who are not elect are condemned and cannot attain salvation, though they are baptized a thousand times, receive the Lord's Supper daily, and live, as much as is possible, holy and blameless lives.

Bibliography

Althaus, Paul. *The Theology of Martin Luther*. Trans. by R.C. Schultz. Philadelphia: Fortress, 1966.

Bateman, Herbert W., ed. *Four Views on the Warning Passages in Hebrews*. Grand Rapids: Kregel, 2007.

Bavinck, Herman. *Reformed Dogmatics*. 3 vols. Edited by John Bolt. Translated by John Vriend. Grand Rapids: Baker Academic, 2004.

Bayer, Oswald. *Martin Luther's Theology: A Contemporary Interpretation*. Translated by Thomas H. Trapp. Grand Rapids: Eerdmans, 2008.

Beasley-Murray, G.R. *Baptism in the New Testament*. Grand Rapids: Eerdmans, 1973.

Bender, Peter C. *Lutheran Catechesis*. 2 ed. Sussex, WI: Concordia Catechetical Academy, 2008.

Bente, F. *Historical Introductions to the Book of Concord*. St. Louis: CPH, 1965.

Bente, F. and Dau, W.H.T., eds. *Concordia Triglotta*. St. Louis: CPH, 1921.

Berkhof, Hendrikus. *Well-Founded Hope*. Richmond, VA: John Knox, 1969.

Berkhof, Louis. *Systematic Theology*. Carlisle, PA: Banner of Truth, 1958.

_____. *The History of Christian Doctrines*. Grand Rapids: Baker, 1937.

Boice, James M. and Ryken, Philip G. *The Doctrines of Grace: Rediscovering the Evangelical Gospel*. Wheaton, IL: Crossway, 2003.

Braaten, Carl E. and Jenson, Robert W., eds. *Christian Dogmatics*. 2 vols. Philadelphia: Fortress, 1984.

Brunner, Emil. *The Letter to the Romans*. Philadelphia: Westminster, 1959.

Byrne, Brendan. *Reckoning with Romans: A Contemporary Reading of Paul's Gospel.* Wilmington, DE: Michael Glazer, 1986.

Calvin, John. *Institutes of the Christian Religion.* Volumes 1–2. Edited by John T. McNeil. Translated by Ford Lewis Battles. Philadelphia: Westminster, 1960.

_____. *Calvin's Commentaries.* 22 vols. Edited and Translated by Joseph Haroutunian. Grand Rapids: Baker Books, 2003.

Cary, Phillip. *Augustine's Invention of the Inner Self: The Legacy of a Christian Platonist.* New York: Oxford University, 2000.

_____. *Outward Signs: The Powerlessness of External Things in Augustine's Thought.* New York: Oxford University, 2008.

_____. "Sola Fide: Luther and Calvin." *CTQ* 71.3 (2007): 265–281.

_____. "Why Luther is Not Quite Protestant: The Logic of Faith in a Sacramental Promise." *Pro Ecclesia* 14.4 (2005): 447–487.

Chemnitz, Martin. *An Enchiridion: Ministry, Word, and Sacraments.* Translated by Luther Poellot. St. Louis: CPH, 1981.

_____. *Loci Theologica.* 2 vols. Translated by J.A.O. Preus. St. Louis: CPH, 1998.

_____. *The Lord's Supper.* Translated by J.A.O. Preus. St. Louis: CPH, 1979.

_____. *The Two Natures of Christ.* Translated by J.A.O. Preus. St. Louis: CPH, 1971.

Cranfield, C.E.B. *Romans: A Shorter Commentary.* Grand Rapids: Eerdmans Publishing, 1987.

Dumbrell, William J. *Romans: A New Covenant Commentary.* Eugene, OR: Wipf and Stock Publishers, 2005.

Ferguson, Sinclair. *Let's Study Ephesians.* Carlisle, PA: Banner of Truth, 2005.

Finn, Thomas M. "The Sacramental World in the Sentences of Peter Lombard." *Theological Studies* 69 (2008): 557–582.

Forde, Gerhard O. *Justification by Faith: A Matter of Death and Life.* Philadelphia: Fortress, 1982.

_____. "Something to Believe: A Theological Perspective on Infant Baptism." *Interpretation* 47 (1993):229–241.

_____. "The Lord's Supper as the Testament of Jesus." *Word and World* 17 (1997): 5–9.

_____. *Theology is for Proclamation.* Minneapolis: Fortress, 1990.

_____. *Where God Meets Man: Luther's Down-to-Earth Approach to the Gospel.* Minneapolis: Augsburg, 1972.

Frame, John M. *Salvation Belongs to the Lord: An Introduction to Systematic Theology.* Phillipsburg, NJ: Presbyterian and Reforemd, 2006.

Gerstner, John H. *Primitive Theology: The Collected Primers.* Carlisle, PA: Soli Deo Gloria, 2003.

Godfrey, Robert. "Calvin on the Eucharist." *Mod Ref* 6.3 (May/June 1997): 48–50.

_____. "Why Baptism?" *Mod Ref* 6.3 (May/June 1997): 27–31.

Graebner, A.L., Dau, W.H.T. and Wessel, Louis. *The Proof Texts of the Catechism with a Practical Commentary.* 2 vols. St. Louis, CPH, 1920.

Grothe, Jonathan F. *The Justification of the Ungodly: An Interpretation of Romans.* 2 vols. Canada: Jonathan F. Grothe, 2005.

Hagner, Donald A. *Encountering Hebrews: An Exposition.* Grand Rapids: Baker, 2002.

Hendriksen, William. *Exposition of the Gospel According to Matthew.* Grand Rapids: Baker, 1982.

_____. *Exposition of Paul's Epistle to the Romans.* Grand Rapids: Baker, 2002.

Hoeneke, Adolf. *Evangelical Lutheran Dogmatics.* 4 vol. Trans. by James Langebartels and Heinrich Vogel. Milwaukee, WI: Northwestern, 2009.

Hohenstein, Herbert H. "A Study of Hebrews 6:4–8." *CTM* 27 (June 1956): 433–444.

Horton, Michael. *The Christian Faith: A Systematic Theology for Pilgrims on the Way.* Grand Rapids: Zondervan, 2010.

_____. *For Calvinism.* Grand Rapids: Zondervan, 2011.

_____. "Union and Communion: Calvin's Theology of Word and Sacrament." *IJST* 11.4 (2009): 398–414.

Hunsinger, George. "The Bread that we Break: Toward a Chalcedonian Resolution of the Eucharist." *Princeton Seminary Bulletin* 24.2 (2003): 241–258.

Jenson, Robert A. *Visible Words: The Interpretation and Practice of Christian Sacraments.* Philadelphia: Fortress, 1978.

Just, Arthur A. Jr. *Luke.* Concordia Commentary. 2 vol. St. Louis: CPH, 1996.

Keener, Craig. *IVP Bible Background Commentary: New Testament.* Downers Grove, IL: IVP Academic, 1994.

Kittel, Gerhard, and Gerhard Friedrich, eds. *Theological Dictionary of the New Testament.* Translated by Geoffrey W. Bromiley. 10 vols. Grand Rapids: Erdmans, 1964–1976.

Koelpin, Arnold J, Ed. *No Other Gospel.* Milwaukee, WI: Northwestern, 1980.

Koester, Craig R. *Symbolism in the Fourth Gospel: Meaning, Mystery, Community.* 2 ed. Minneapolis: Fortress, 2003.

Kolb, Robert. *The Christian Faith: A Lutheran Exposition.* St. Louis, CPH, 1993.

Kolb, Robert and Arand, Charles P. *The Genius of Luther's Theology.* Grand Rapids: Baker, 2008.

Kolb, Robert and Wengert, Timothy J., eds. *The Book of Concord: The Confessions of the Evangelical Lutheran Church.* Minneapolis: Fortress, 2000.

Krauth, Charles P. *The Conservative Reformation and Its Theology.* St. Louis: CPH, 2007.

Lenski R.C.H. *Lenski's Commentary on the New Testament.* 20 vol. Minneapolis: Augsburg Fortress, 2008.

Leithart, Peter J. *The Baptized Body.* Moscow, ID: Canon, 2007.

Luther, Martin. *The Bondage of the Will.* Translated by J.I. Packer and O.R. Johnston. Grand Rapids: Baker Academic, 2012.

_____. *Complete Sermons of Martin Luther.* 4 vols. Grand Rapids: Baker, 2000.

_____. *Luther's Works.* 55 vols. American Edition. Edited by Jaroslav Pelikan and Helmut T. Lehmann. St. Louis: CPH, 1958.

Lull, Timothy F., ed. *Martin Luther's Basic Theological Writings.* Minneapolis: Fortress, 1989.

Mathison, Keith A. *Given for You: Reclaiming Calvin's Doctrine of the Lord's Supper.* Phillipsburg, NJ: Presbyterian and Reformed, 2002.

McCain, Paul T., ed. *Concordia: The Lutheran Confessions.* St. Louis: CPH, 2005.

McGrath, Alister E. *Iustitia Dei: A History of the Christian Doctrine of Justification.* Cambridge: Cambridge University, 1986.

_____. *Reformation Thought: An Introduction.* Second Edition. Oxford: Blackwell, 1993.

_____. *Spirituality in an Age of Change: Rediscovering the Spirit of the Reformers*. Grand Rapids: Zondervan, 1994.

McKnight, Scot. "The Warning Passages of Hebrews: A Formal Analysis and Theological Conclusions." *Trinity Journal* 13 (1992): 21–59.

Melanchthon, Phillip. *Loci Communes* (1543). Edited and Translated by J.A.O Preus. St. Louis: CPH, 1992.

Moldstad, J.A. "The Inspired Paradigm for Presenting the Doctrine of Election." S.T.M. Thesis, Wisconsin Lutheran Seminary, 2002.

Moo, Douglas J. *The Epistle to the Romans*. New International Commentary on the New Testament. Grand Rapids: Eerdmans, 1996.

Morris, Leon. *The Gospel According to John*. Rev. ed. Grand Rapids: Eerdmans, 1995.

Mueller, John T. *Christian Dogmatics*. St. Louis: CPH, 2003.

Mueller, Steven P., ed. *Called to Believe, Teach, and Confess: An Introduction to Doctrinal Theology*. Eugene, OR: Wipf and Stock, 2005.

Muller, Richard A. "Calvin on Sacramental Presence, in the Shadow of Marburg and Zurich." *LQ* 23 (2009): 147–167.

_____. *Dictionary of Latin and Greek Theological Terms: Drawn Largely from Protestant Scholastic Theology*. Grand Rapids: Baker, 1985.

Murray, John. *Christian Baptism*. Philadelphia: Presbyterian and Reformed, 1972.

_____. *Collected Writings of John Murray*. 4 vols. Carlisle: PA, Banner of Truth, 1996.

_____. *Epistle to the Romans*. Grand Rapids: Eerdmans, 1968.

_____. *Redemption: Accomplished and Applied*. Carlisle, PA: Banner of Truth Trust, 1961.

Nagel, Norman. *Selected Sermons of Norman Nagel: From Valparaiso to St. Louis*. St. Louis: CPH, 2004.

Neve, J.L. *A History of Christian Thought*. 2 vol. Philadelphia: Muhlenberg, 1946.

Nygren, Anders. *Commentary on Romans*. Translated by Carl C. Rasmussen. Philadelphia: Muhlenberg, 1949.

Owen, John. *The Death of Death in the Death of Christ*. Carlisle, PA: Banner of Truth Trust, 1995.

Palmer, Edwin. *The Five Points of Calvinism*. Grand Rapids: Baker, 1972.

Paulson, Steven D. *Lutheran Theology*. London: T&T Clark, 2011.

Pieper, Francis. *Christian Dogmatics*. 3 vols. St. Louis: CPH, 1953.

Pless, John T. *Martin Luther: Preacher of the Cross*. St. Louis: CPH, 2013.

Plummer, Alfred. *The Pastoral Epistles*. 3d ed. London: Hodder and Stoughton, 1889.

Prenter, Regin. *More about Luther*. 2 vols. Decorah, IA: Luther College, 1958.

Preus, Herman A. *A Theology to Live By: The Practical Luther for the Practicing Christian*. St. Louis, CPH, 1977.

Preus, Jacob A.O. *Just Words: Understanding the Fullness of the Gospel*. St. Louis, CPH, 2000.

Preus, Robert D. *Getting into the Theology of Concord: A Study of the Book of Concord*. St. Louis: CPH, 1977.

Reu, Johann M. *Lutheran Dogmatics*. 2 vol. Dubuque, IA: Wartburg Theological Seminary, 1951.

_____. *Two Treatises on the Means of Grace*. Minneapolis: Augsburg, 1952.

Ridderbos, Herman N. *The Epistle of Paul to the Churches of Galatia*. Grand Rapids: Eerdmans, 1953.

Rogers, Cleon Jr., and Cleon Rogers III. *The New Linguistic and Exegetical Key to the Greek New Testament*. Grand Rapids: Zondervan, 1998.

Rohls, Jan. *Reformed Confessions: Theology from Zurich to Barmen*. Translated by John F. Hoffmeyer. Louisville, KY: WJK, 1998.

Ryken, Leland, James C. Wilhoit, and Tremper Longman III, eds. *Dictionary of Biblical Imagery*. Downers Grove, IL: InterVarsity, 1998.

Ryle, J.C. *Expository Thoughts on the Gospels*. 4 vol. Carlisle, PA: Banner of Truth, 1985.

Sasse, Hermann. *This is My Body: Luther's Contention for the Real Presence in the Sacrament of the Altar*. St. Louis: CPH, 2003.

Scaer, David. "Nature and Extent of the Atonement in Lutheran Theology." *BETS* 10.4 (Fall 1967):179–187.

_____. "Reformed Exegesis and Lutheran Sacraments." *CTQ* 64.1 (Jan 2000): 3–20.

_____. "The Holy Spirit, Sacraments, and Church Rites." *CTQ* 70.3/4 (2006): 311–322.

Schaller, John. *Biblical Christology: A Study in Lutheran Dogmatics.* Milwaukee, WI: Northwestern, 1981.

Schmemann, Alexander. *The Eucharist.* Yonkers, NY: St. Vladimir's Seminary Press, 2003.

Senkbeil, Harold L. *Dying to Live: The Power of Forgiveness.* St Louis, CPH, 1994.

Sproul, R.C. *1–2 Peter: St. Andrew's Expositional Commentary.* Wheaton: Crossway, 2011.

_____. *Can I Be Sure I'm Saved?* Sanford, FL: Reformation Trust, 2010.

_____. *Chosen by God.* Wheaton: Tyndale House, 1986.

_____. *Grace Unknown: The Heart of Reformed Theology.* Grand Rapids: Baker, 1997.

_____. *Matthew: St. Andrew's Expositional Commentary.* Wheaton: Crossway, 2013.

_____. *Romans: St. Andrew's Expositional Commentary.* Wheaton: Crossway, 2009.

_____. *Truths We Confess: A Layman's Guide to the Westminster Confession of Faith.* 3 vols. Phillipsburg, NJ: Presbyterian and Reformed, 2006.

_____. *What is Baptism?* Sanford, FL: Reformation Trust, 2011.

_____. *What is the Lord's Supper?* Sanford, FL. Reformation Trust, 2013.

_____. *What is Reformed Theology: Understanding the Basics.* Grand Rapids: Baker Books, 1997.

Spitz, Lewis W. *Renaissance and Reformation Movements.* 2 vols. St. Louis: CPH, 1971.

Steele, David N. and Thomas, Curtis C. *The Five Points of Calvinism: Defined, Defended, Documented.* Phillipsburg, NJ: Presbyterian and Reformed, 1963.

Stephenson, John R. *The Lord's Supper.* Confessional Lutheran Dogmatics, Vol. 12. St. Louis: Luther Academy, 2003.

Tappert, Theodore, ed. *Luther's Letters of Spiritual Counsel.* Philadelphia: Westminster, 1955.

Teigen, Bjarne W. *I Believe: A Study of the Formula of Concord.* Mankato, MN: Bethany Lutheran College, 1977.

Thelemann, Otto. *An Aid to the Heidelberg Catechism.* Translated by M. Peters. Grand Rapids: Douma Publications, 1959.

Thomas, Derek W.H. *Acts: Reformed Expository Commentary*. Phillipsburg, NJ: Presbyterian and Reformed, 2011.

Tobin, Thomas H. *Paul's Rhetoric in its Contexts: The Argument of Romans*. Grand Rapids: Baker, 2005.

Trigg, Jonathan. *Baptism in the Theology of Martin Luther*. New York: E.J. Brill, 1994.

Vanhoozer, Kevin. *The Drama of Doctrine: A Canonical Linguistic Approach to Christian Theology*. Louisville, KY: WJK, 2005.

Walther, C.F.W. *Selected Writings*. 6 vol. St. Louis: CPH, 1981.

Westerholm, Stephen. *Understanding Paul: The Early Christian Worldview of the Letter to the Romans*. 2 ed. Grand Rapids: Baker Academic, 2004.

Zahl, Paul. *Grace in Practice: A Theology of Everyday Life*. Grand Rapids: Eerdmans, 2007.

Scripture Index

Made in the USA
Middletown, DE
19 February 2016